# God at the Speed of Light

# God at the Speed of Light

## The Melding of Science and Spirituality

by T. Lee Baumann, M.D.

ARE
PRESS

**ASSOCIATION FOR
RESEARCH AND
ENLIGHTENMENT**

A.R.E. Press • Virginia Beach • Virginia

A.R.E. Press
215 67th Street
Virginia Beach, VA 23451-2061

Baumann, T. Lee, 1950-
God at the speed of light : the melding of science and spirituality / by T. Lee Baumann.
    p.    cm.
Includes bibliographical references and index.
    ISBN 0-87604-439-9
    1. Religion and Science. 2. Near-death experiences. 3. Precognition. 4. Miracles. I. Title.
    BL240.3.B382002
    291.1'75—dc21

                                    2002016393

Cover design by Richard Boyle

*This book is dedicated to my beloved family and friends,
who served as the catalysts for this text.*

# Contents:

# Acknowledgments

The author is grateful for permission to use excerpts from the following works:

*After the Light*, Kimberly Clark Sharp. © 1995 by Kimberly Clark Sharp. Reprinted by permission of HarperCollins Publishers, Inc. William Morrow.

*Closer to the Light*, Melvin Morse, M.D., and Paul Perry. © 1998 by Melvin Morse, M.D., and Paul Perry. Reprinted by permission of Ballantine Books, a Division of Random House, Inc.

*Fire in the Mind*, George Johnson. © 1995 by George Johnson. Reprinted by permission of Alfred A. Knopf, a division of Random House, Inc.

*In Search of Schrodinger's Cat*, John Gribbin. © 1984 by John and Mary Gribbin. Used by permission of Bantam Books, a division of Random House, Inc.

*Merriam-Webster's Collegiate Dictionary, Tenth Edition*. By permission. *Merriam-Webster's Collegiate® Dictionary, Tenth Edition* ©2000 by Merriam-Webster, Inc.

*People of the Lie*, M. Scott Peck, M.D. © 1983 by M. Scott Peck. Reprinted with the permission of Simon and Schuster.

*Quantum Reality: Beyond the New Physics*, Nick Herbert. © 1985 by Nick Herbert. Used by permission of Doubleday, a division of Random House, Inc.

*Revised Standard Version of the Bible*. © 1952 by the Division of Christian Education of the National Council of the Churches of Christ in the United States of America. Used by Permission. All rights reserved.

*Schrodinger's Kitten's and the Search for Reality*, John Gribbin. © 1995 by John and Mary Gribbin. By permission of Little, Brown and Company (Inc.). [U.K. Weidenfeld & Nicholson]

*Self-Aware Universe*, Amit Goswami and Maggie

# Preface

As with many of my readers, I began formulating questions about life at an early age. My brothers and I grew up with a great respect for my parents and were raised under the influence of their beliefs, including religion. As children, we accepted these beliefs and attitudes without question. With the protection extended by their sustenance, shelter, care, and love, our parents led us to believe, with equal faith, that God would extend to us the same courtesy. As I entered adulthood, questions arose that caused me to question these doctrines and to search for a verification of these ideals with my changing attitudes.

As time progressed, I developed a great respect and appreciation for the tenets of scientific research, as experienced through my education in biology, chemistry, pre-med and, finally, medicine. Questions continued, however, relative to God, miracles (including those I witnessed firsthand in my medical practice), and the apparent infinity and design of the universe. My admiration of medicine and the incredulity of life led me through a natural progression to investigate the nature of humankind and its role in the universe.

The theory of evolution was one of the first stepping-stones in this developmental process. Unfortunately, it also represented one of the greatest obstacles to my religious heritage. I would ultimately learn that the questions this theory inspired were only part of a normal path of spiritual growth. Scott Peck, M.D., has identified a four-stage process of spiritual growth (see Chapter 7).[i] Little did I know that I was passing through a normal phase of my own religious development.

Many questions continued unanswered through the succeeding years, which now found me preparing for graduation from my medical residency and inauguration into the world of medical practice. At about this time, I read and was mesmerized by Raymond Moody, M.D.'s bestseller[ii] on the descriptions of patients surviving what came to be called near-death experiences or NDEs. This was my first reading of a scientific attestation of a phenomenon which, though indistinguishable (as depicted by the victims) from supernatural occurrences, could not be arbitrarily dismissed by the scientific community. I felt spiritually rejuvenated, but lingering doubts persisted.

I had previously noted my awe with the surrounding universe, such as when I viewed the nighttime sky. The universe appeared infinite in its dimensions, and I was convinced of the insignificance of humanity. I questioned whether the human race had any true purpose in such a world. If a Supreme or Designing Being really existed, why did He not make His presence known? I felt like an orphan without a father. Of course, I was not alone in these thoughts.

I was vaguely familiar with Einstein and his theories of relativity, including the relationships of energy to matter and light ($E = mc^2$). How could energy, with the work and heat associated with the various forces and matter, be just another form of those same things? I decided to familiarize myself with this concept.

$E=mc^2$ soon led to my introduction to quantum physics and quantum theory. Around 1980, I was intrigued by Nigel Calder's introduction to the theories of relativity, presented in simple layman's terms.[iii] Following this fascinating journey into Einstein's life, I pursued more on the subject in the strangely titled *The Dancing Wu Li Masters* by Gary Zukav.[iv] This book initiated my research of the "new" physics as a possible scientific window that might unite many vague concepts of science and religion. I read more . . . and more . . . and more.

Quantum theory, dealing with explanations of everything from atoms to black holes, seemed to have irrefutable support from the scientific community. In addition, I was struck with the fact that many of these scientists believed in God. It appeared that their profession often enhanced their belief in a Designing Being, rather than diminishing it. My own plunge into quantum theory convinced me of God's existence and verified many of those early religious doctrines that I had called into question.

Concomitant with my study of quantum theory, the scientific literature began to reveal evidence of the failings of the theory of evolution. The evidence was mounting!

Scientists have, over the last many years, been making slow but steady progress in revealing the true nature of the universe, including the confirmation of *design* in its character and the importance of our species. The scientific evidence in support of a designing force as the prime mover in our universe is becoming extensive. In contrast, there is a great paucity of supporting literature available to the lay public.

It is evident that history, as well as my own spiritual growth, have come full circle. As late as the mid-1900s, religious attitudes were supported mostly on faith. Over the succeeding decades, acceptance of the theory of evolution and ongoing scientific research appeared to refute many religious dogmas. However, over this same period of time, the popularization of Albert Einstein's theories of relativity and the subsequent acceptance of the Big Bang theory began to gain the attention of the lay public. Quantum physics has recently evolved to support the creation of the universe "from nothing," the story of Genesis in the Bible, free will, and *some* supernatural phenomena. In addition, the inexplicable characteristics of light have incredible comparisons to God.

Lastly, the *soul* has gained scientific credence as portrayed by Moody's near-death revelations,[v] quantum theory's proofs regarding "observation," and the exceptional status of humanity in the universe.

As I first verbalized to the initial reviewers of my book, "I am not a religious fanatic." Rather, this book represents my attempt to avail this extraordinary information to the general public. The information presented here is inspiring, fulfilling, and should provide answers to many of the questions that we have all sought on life's many mysteries.

# 1

# Adventures in Death

I anticipated no book more eagerly than Raymond Moody's *Life After Life*,[1] a nonfiction documentary detailing the experiences of people who had suffered cardiac arrests. My own experiences in medicine led me to believe that death was more than just a return of the body to "dust." Unfortunately, medicine and the scientific principles in which I had been trained offered little in the way of any explanation.

During the majority of cardiopulmonary resuscitations (CPRs), victims are truly lifeless. Airways are placed through the mouth or nose, needles are inserted into the extremities and heart, medications are administered, and, all the while, trained personnel administer cardiac massage to an already traumatized heart.

During my medical residency, all hospital personnel were trained to perform CPR. In practice, residents and interns performed the vast majority of resuscitations. "Code Blue" announcements throughout the hospital communicated the event. Nurses from the floor and all physicians (in training or otherwise) responded. The scene was one of initial chaos. The first staff to arrive initiated cardiac massage and ventilation. Nurses started intravenous (IV) lines. Anesthesia staff or emergency doctors placed airways. One doctor read from the chart and gleaned any useful information. The highest-ranking doctor assumed the lead. Everyone fulfilled a vital function. Nevertheless, the life forms beneath our hands reacted as bodies in suspended animation. The staff was always professional, but the situation lacked reality. At times, our actions appeared in slow motion, like scenes from a movie. There was an aura of surrealism. Something unaccounted for transpired that no one could explain. Everyone performed, from his or her "cookbook," the automatic routine for saving a life—but we were not in control. Perhaps the surreal feeling was because we had acted out this scenario before and knew that our efforts might end in vain. Or, perhaps, it was the older attending physician who cautioned us to "be careful what you say" during the resuscitation. He believed some victims were aware of our actions and conversation. Of course, this was impossible. These patients were unconscious, or beyond. No one seriously believed the elder doctor—then.

And we all had cases we couldn't explain. I remember being called to pronounce someone's death, an official part of the death certification. Some patients escape having to undergo CPR because they have chronic, incurable, or, otherwise terminal conditions. Old age is the most common of these conditions. In this instance, I took the elevator to the floor. I surveyed the chart as I walked slowly into the room, observing the drawn curtains around the bed. The gentleman lay peacefully; there were no signs of the often-futile efforts of a failed resuscitation attempt. I pulled the stethoscope from my coat, and verified the absence of *both* heartbeat and breath sounds. Medical training teaches us to take nothing for granted. Indeed, the nurses were right about his status, as they usually were, having more experience in these matters than the young medical interns. I "pronounced" this elderly man, verified the time of death on the death certificate and medical record, and proceeded with my hospital rounds. There were no living relatives to notify. I will never forget the phone call I received thirty minutes later from the nursing station of that floor I had just left: Did I know that the man I had pronounced was now awake and alert? Surely there was some mistake, I said. But it turned out to be very true. I stared at the phone in disbelief and then ran to see for myself.

Astounded, I found him talking, responsive, and back to his normal self to boot. At best, I would have expected to see some brain damage from lack of adequate circulation for such a prolonged period, certainly in excess of thirty minutes. I was glad to be wrong. He was fine. In retrospect, he conceivably had extremely low blood pressure and shallow, intermittent breathing (so as to be undetectable) to explain my previous findings. However, I would have—or *should have*—heard heart sounds (which is why we check *both* the heart and lungs), but I heard no heart sounds. This man had been clinically dead. Now, he was alive.

Life is indeed strange and inexplicable.

And then there are the successful resuscitations. These individuals regain consciousness after CPR, attached to a ventilator, frightened, and unable to speak. The patients struggle to communicate, but can't. They are restrained, in extreme pain, and in a state of added confusion from any sedation. The multiple tubes compound the terror.

Awaking in an ICU can be a horrifying experience: many new and strange faces, often with masks; gowns; bloody gloves; needles; and lines, like scenes from a nightmare. There are equally terrifying sounds: constant voices, shouting, crashing of carts, beeping and humming of monitors and ventilators—twenty-four hours a day— never-ending. The smell of sterility fills the air.

Understandably, the experience transforms the individual. Most physicians attribute the patients' metamorphoses to the result of sleep deprivation, fear of impending death, medications, confusion, and pain. Of course, there are those patients who are thankful and grateful to be alive, with many things yet to complete in their lives. There are those who are repentant and plan to correct their lives. Then, there are those who are angry— to be alive. This may initially appear to be a surprising finding, but chronically ill patients familiar with hospitals' emergency departments have commonly expressed such feelings. Why did hospital personnel interfere, only to prolong their suffering? The emergency staff who routinely snatch lives from the grips of Death are frequently the targets of such complaints. These patients do not fear death. Rather, they maintain that these well-intentioned people delayed their inevitable passage to a better, or at least less painful, world. For them, a contrasting perspective has replaced what, in youth, was once a will to live. Hospital experiences and end-of-life tribulations can alter behaviors and attitudes toward life.

Prior to Moody's book, few physicians entertained the notion that at least some of these patients might have experienced something on the order of divine intervention. When Life After Life was published, many of the stories I heard patients relate, following their near-death experiences, suddenly gained substance and credibility. Dr. Moody is a physician with both an M.D. degree and a Ph.D. in philosophy. His book was matter-of-fact, believable, unbiased, and consistent with my medical experience.

In the typical near-death experience (NDE), Dr. Moody found several common elements[2] in a relative order. A characteristic example may include the following:

1. Apparent death
2. Separation from the body
3. Travel through a dark tunnel
4. Greetings by deceased loved ones and friends
5. Pervading feelings of warmth, peace, and love
6. Encounter with a "being of light"
7. A life review
8. Communication that the victim must return to the living; disappointment
9. Reunion with the physical body
10. Difficulty in describing the episode
11. Disbelief by others; abandonment of further attempts to relate the experience
12. Changed perspective on life

Several similar publications by physicians followed, both in prestigious medical journals as well as in book form. I was intrigued by the sudden awareness in the medical community that medicine now apparently competed with an unknown power in these cases. Doctors and scientists offered several hypotheses to explain the occurrences. The most common rationales included possible effects of drugs and/or oxygen deprivation. However, for every argument, there was a multitude of cases where such justifications did not pertain. People were found to recount similar near-death visions who were under surgery (receiving oxygen and ventilatory support prior to CPR), in the ICU (where CPR initiation and oxygen administration were immediate), or otherwise in the hospital (where rapid treatment was instituted). The technique of CPR is quite effective. I can recount one of several cases I witnessed where the individual was responsive only as long as CPR was in progress. Likewise, when the staff temporarily stopped CPR (e.g., for placement of a tracheal airway), the person relapsed into unconsciousness. Again, when the staff resumed resuscitation, the victim became responsive. As Dr. Moody described, "during resuscitation procedures, the brain is being perfused with blood and with the oxygen and nourishment it carries. This is the point of cardiac massage: to keep the blood flowing even though the heart is not beating by itself."[3]

My wife also happens to be a physician, board-certified in the specialties of family practice and emergency medicine. We have had many discussions regarding her personal observations of near-death phenomena. Over her twenty-five years of practice, she and her colleagues in the ER have had countless conversations about the similarities of their patients' anecdotes and the NDE elements related by Moody. Descriptions of "light, warmth, love, peace" were not uncommon. As previously noted, not only were some patients upset over the obtrusion into their deaths, but several *knew* that death was immediately forthcoming anyway. In these cases, nothing the doctors and nurses did was going to prevent death, only postpone it for a short time. Indeed, these individuals seemed to have an uncanny awareness of their limited time on this Earth. One example was that of a young, previously healthy man hit by a car. When evaluated in the ER, he had a low blood pressure, but his other vital signs were normal. As he was being prepared for treatment and the intravenous lines, he remarked, "Nothing you do is going to make any difference. I'm dying." He died a short time later despite all the available miracles of modern medicine. At autopsy, he had an unusual tear of a coronary artery, an artery which supplies needed blood and oxygen to the heart. Was this patient just young and frightened as a result of the accident, or did he *really know* he was about to die—and how did he know?

Another example is the case of a man with recurrent ventricular tachycardia, a life-threatening heart irregularity. While in the ICU, his therapy was not successful. CPR occurred repeatedly, since this arrhythmia does not provide adequate circulation. After several days of suffering this torment, he reported to his physicians, "I've seen Jesus. I'm not afraid. I wish you'd just let me go." He also described seeing "the light."

The old or infirm are not the only ones to experience the peace and exhilaration of the NDE. The healthy, young, and happy equally express this view, as illustrated by a soon-to-be-married twenty-two-year-old:

> Again, without words, I learned that I had to return to my life on earth. I was appalled. Leave all this . . . ? No way. The girl who always did as she was told dug in her heels. But to no avail. I was going back.[4] (Sharp)

I suspect that most physicians encounter stories of this type from time to time from their patients. Perhaps they believe the accounts; perhaps they discount them as coming from individuals under duress. I was especially intrigued by observations of an atheist colleague and friend who worked the ER. He was mystified by the accounts of patients who related encounters with light and love, who no longer feared death, and who were annoyed at the interference of the medical personnel trying to forestall the inevitable.

Victims of NDEs less commonly report negative experiences. These encounters may involve darkness, instead of light, and demons and Satan, instead of angels and God:

Howard Storm . . . was hospitalized with a perfo-
rated duodenum [ulcer]. The pain became so great
that Howard left his body and observed it lying in
bed, his wife seated next to him. Unable to get her
attention, he followed some beings who looked like
humans, beckoning to him. He followed them into a
foggy realm that grew progressively darker. Then
they revealed themselves as demonic beings who
attacked him. To his surprise, Howard discovered
that saying words with religious implications, such
as God would frighten the creatures away. Alone in
the darkness and in despair, he cried out, "Jesus,
please save me!" Such an exhortation was unlike
Howard, who described himself as a resolute atheist, someone who believed that he, not God, was the
center of the universe.

As soon as Howard called out for help, a Light
came down from above, lifting him up. Howard's
experience then took on the nature of a positive
near-death experience. He found himself surrounded by loving spiritual beings and saw a review of his life, which he observed had been almost
entirely self-serving . . .

Today, he is a minister of a church in Cincinnati.[5]
(Sharp)

Another area of fascination involves unexplained visions, which are later *corroborated* by friends or relatives.
By this, I am including such perceptions as predeath visions, visions of the future, and "out-of-body" experiences (including descriptions of the details of their
resuscitation and witnessed events outside the hospital).
Moody summarized, "Numerous persons have told me
that while they were out of their bodies during apparent
'death,' they witnessed events at a distance—even
outside the hospital—which were later confirmed by

the reports of independent observers."[6]

Dr. Melvin Morse, a pediatrician who writes of near-death experiences of children,[7] revealed numerous corroborated accounts of out-of-body experiences. Examples include a patient who identified a shoe on the hospital ledge, far outside her hospital window and beyond possible viewing, and multiple descriptions of patients depicting their resuscitations with great precision. One teenage girl (near-death researcher Michelle Sorensen, who now has published as well) foresaw her future family during her out-of-body journey, including an accurate vision of her future husband's height and hair color, and identification of her two children, a son and daughter.[8]

One particularly interesting case[9] involved a man struck by a car. Similar to the previously mentioned case in which I was involved, Yuri was pronounced dead and actually taken to the hospital morgue. He recalled lying on the cold, metal autopsy table, waiting for the pathologist who would perform the autopsy. During this time, Yuri "found himself surrounded by light," and traveled to see his grieving wife and family. He even visited the neighbors, and noted, "I could talk to the baby. It was amazing." He found, interestingly, that he could not communicate with anyone else. This infant was just recently born and had been irritable since his birth. No one had been able to determine the cause of the baby's distress: "[The baby] told me that his arm hurt. And when he told me that, I was able to see that the bone was twisted and broken." Unbelievably, Yuri remained in cold storage at the morgue for three days. When the pathologist finally arrived to perform the autopsy, he noticed movement of Yuri's eyes. After a more thorough examination, the doctor found his subject to be quite alive, and rushed him to emergency surgery. Yuri's recount of his adventure was met with skepticism until he provided detailed descriptions of his observations, including his interaction with the neighbors' baby. Based on the now-conscious Yuri's report, the parents took the child to the doctor for an X-ray, which confirmed the missed diagnosis of a broken arm.

Erma, a close relative of mine, also had an NDE. She was involved in a terrible automobile accident and taken by ambulance to the nearest hospital. She recalls hovering over her body while the doctors and nurses worked on her resuscitation. Her case seemed futile, and Erma remembers a nurse removing her dentures. As her teeth were thrown into the trash, the nurse remarked, "She won't be needing these anymore!" Following her recovery, Erma described the resuscitation in great detail to her family. Her daughter was especially fascinated and went to the point of corroborating the denture story with the nurse in the ER!

The literature is now teeming with anecdotes of near-death experiences. Nearly everyone is familiar with them and, possibly, have heard firsthand accounts.

In looking back through history, we see that ancient cultures are replete with death chronicles. Examples include The Egyptian Book of the Dead (1500 B.C.), The Tibetan Book of the Dead (also known as the Bardo Thödol, eighth century A.D.), the Aztec Song of the Dead, and the writings of Plato (428-348 B.C.) and Emanuel Swedenborg (1688-1772).

The Egyptian Book of the Dead and The Tibetan Book of the Dead are similar in that both serve to lead the dead or dying through and beyond death.[10] Rituals are performed to aid the newly dead in the transition to a new existence. The newly deceased are then judged by a symbolic weighing of their virtuous vs. corrupt deeds in life.[11] Those failing the judgment are either devoured (Egyptian) or led away to a Hell-equivalent (Tibetan). In The Tibetan Book of the Dead,[12] the deceased may have great difficulty realizing that they are dead. The adversity that each experiences in this transition will decide whether the soul is liberated by an entity of "Clear Light" (achievement of the supreme state of *Nirvana*) or destined for Heaven or Hell. Neither Heaven nor Hell, however, is permanent. After the due reward or punishment, as the case may be, the dead are reincarnated with new existences on Earth. This cycle may be ever repeated. Hence, the Tibetan believes that all living beings have returned from death. Reincarnation as a human is considered the ultimate privilege, since only this opportunity offers the possibility for liberation of the soul, or Nirvana. The exact dating of these Tibetan rituals is unknown, having been passed orally from generation to generation prior to being finally recorded in the eighth century A.D.

Plato,[13] in both his *Phaedo* and *The Republic*, discussed death and the soul. In *Phaedo*, Plato described a soldier who was slain in battle and was taken home for burial after lying, presumed dead, on the battlefield for ten days. As his body was being prepared for burial, he regained consciousness and told of his near-death experience. His soul had left his body and traveled "to a mysterious place." He met with other beings, who told him that he was to serve as a "messenger," to report his experience in this other world. His experience included encounters with light and Heaven, and, eventually, the return to his body.[14]

And what of the Bible? Research reveals that there are many biblical references to resurrection of the body following death, most notably, that of Christ following his crucifixion:

> They were at the tomb early in the morning and did not find his body; and they came back saying that they had even seen a vision of angels, who said that he was alive. Luke 24:22-23, Revised Standard Version (RSV)

And as they were saying this, Jesus himself stood among them . . .

"See my hands and my feet, that it is I myself; handle me, and see; for a spirit has not flesh and bones as you see that I have." Luke 24:36-39 (RSV)

Another celebrated "near-death" narrative is that of Lazarus:

Jesus said, "Take away the stone." Martha, the sister of the dead man, said to him, "Lord, by this time there will be an odor, for he has been dead four days."

Jesus said unto her, "Did I not tell you that if you would believe you would see the glory of God?"

So they took away the stone. And Jesus lifted up his eyes and said, "Father, I thank thee that thou hast heard me . . ."

When he had said this, he cried with a loud voice, "Lazarus, come out."

The dead man came out, his hands and feet bound with bandages, and his face wrapped with a cloth. Jesus said to them, "Unbind him, and let him go." John 11:39-44 (RSV)

There exist many parallels in these various texts with Moody's description of the NDE, including the presence of guides and/or guardian spirits; an omnipotent light, uncertainty over one's death, separation from the body, a review of life's events, judgment; clearness of thought and perception; and/or feelings of peace, love, and contentment.

There are other death-related visions as well. In this category, I'm including predeath visions experienced by those about to die, as well as visions by close relatives.

In an example cited by Melvin Morse, M.D., a couple,

Edna and Tom, were coping with their daughter's battle against breast cancer. Everyone remained optimistic, despite the cancer's relentless progression. Chemotherapy continued:

The night after their daughter's chemotherapy, Tom woke up to see his daughter standing at the foot of his bed. She was dressed in white and glowing brightly. She sat at the foot of the bed and talked to her father. He couldn't understand anything she said but he felt a deep sense of peace at seeing her so "dressed up." Tom immediately awoke Edna. He was wide awake and talking fast about what he had just seen. Edna didn't question whether it was a dream. Both of them knew what it meant. Their daughter had died. In a few hours they received a call . . . telling them what they already knew.[15]

Predeath visions are some of the more striking descriptions in the literature. Nightmarish features often characterize these accounts. In the next example, a boy began to have a recurring dream, two months before his death. He described the repeating scenario to his mother and sketched several images recalled from the dream. A "glowing princess" forewarned him of his imminent death. In another scene from the dream, all the doors closed, blocking his path, except one. He sketched visions of a tall monument and a distinctive-looking tree:

Two days before he was shot, the boy went for a walk with his mother. He took her hand and said in the most serious of tones: "If I die, don't cry about it. I know I'm going to be happy there because they showed me. It's beautiful."

Linda was shocked. She asked him pointedly if he was thinking of committing suicide, which he denied. "I just don't think I'm going to be here much longer."

. . . On the night her son was shot, Linda awoke with a backache. She sat up with a start and began to cry. She said her upper back hurt and she was afraid something awful had happened. When the phone rang a few minutes later, Linda stood up and screamed, "My son is dead," before her husband picked up the receiver and heard the bad news from the police.

When they buried the boy a few days later, both Linda and her husband noticed something they had seen on his drawing pads. The tall monument from a neighboring grave was the same as in his pictures. The same . . . about the tree at the gravesite.[16] (Morse)

This boy was accidentally shot at a party. A girl had found the gun and, not knowing if it were real, fired the gun outside, into the air. Concluding that the gun was a toy, the girl handed it, barrel first, to Linda's son; the gun went off in the process. Certainly, this was a great tragedy. However, it is noteworthy that the boy was not an active participant in the calamity; i.e., the premonition could not have been operative as a self-fulfilling prophecy, as has been argued in some cases. This feature lends credence to the legitimacy of the predeath vision as a special phenomenon.

Social worker-turned author, Kimberly Clark Sharp,[17] related the circumstances surrounding her own fiancé's untimely death, which she witnessed in a vision:

It took the emergency personnel a while to find George's body. He had been thrown into a snowbank and was buried in the snow. His body was found as I had seen it in my vision six hours before the van left the road. I had seen it, but I couldn't prevent it. No one could.[18]

It is unusual for these visions to extend beyond the realm of the intended recipient. Here is one case, reported by researchers Karlis Osis and Erlendur Haraldsson, where some of the energy escaped into the common domain:

> He was unsedated, fully conscious, and had a low temperature. . . In the room where he was lying, there was a staircase leading to the second floor. Suddenly he exclaimed: "See, the angels are coming down the stairs. The glass has fallen and broken." All of us in the room looked toward the staircase where a drinking glass had been placed on one of the steps. As we looked, we saw the glass break into a thousand pieces without any apparent cause. It did not fall; it simply exploded. The angels, of course, we did not see. A happy and peaceful expression came over the patient's face, and the next moment he expired.[19]

I have intentionally tried to be very selective in the cases I have reprinted here. I have not listed numerous other accounts, which are essentially repetitious, and I have omitted some very impressive experiences that might be considered the direct result of certain illnesses; e.g., ailments involving the brain, or the circulation or oxygenation of blood to the brain.

Close friends and relatives have also experienced predeath visions, which greatly affected members of my own family.

Uncle Turk was a simple but kind man, in his seventies. He and his wife, Erma (the same as discussed previously), lived for their family. It was typical of their household to arrange for twenty-four hour, around-the-clock vigils of any relative in the hospital, no matter how minor the illness. I had always been impressed by such dedication. Fortunately, they had quite a large family, but filling all the "shifts" was still a considerable challenge. During serious and protracted illnesses, relatives would come to Tennessee from as far away as Ohio, Florida, and Alabama to cover all the time slots. I give this historical background only to demonstrate the unusual closeness of this family.

One morning, Uncle Turk related how he had had a dream. Their son, Pete, deceased for several years, had appeared before him. "It won't be long before I see you, Dad," Pete had told him. Uncle Turk had no doubt the vision was real. This dream repeated itself on several more occasions. Turk asked his brother-in-law to drive him to many locations where he wished to recall fond memories. He wanted to view them one last time. During this time, he prepared for his death, even though his health appeared good. Uncle Turk died several weeks later of a sudden heart attack, collapsing on his way to the bathroom.

More than ten years after his death, Turk visited Erma in a dream. "I'll be seeing you soon, Honey," he told her. Erma began to prepare for her own death. During this time, Pete also visited her in a dream and told her that it wouldn't be long until they were all together. Within six months, Erma had also passed away.

Certainly, the case can be argued that, perhaps, their deaths were the result of self-fulfilling prophecies, triggered by the dreams. However, my own experience as a physician reminds me of how resilient the human body is. There is a sense in the medical community that people can effect their own deaths, provided there is a true death wish, *concomitant* with a death-defining illness. Neither

Turk nor Erma wanted death. They still enjoyed life and their children and grandchildren. They still led active and productive lives and were mentally alert and stable. Neither did they fear death; they accepted it as fact. I personally do not feel that the dreams initiated a self-fulfilling cycle toward death, but, rather, that some external force was at play.

Danny was only eight years old when he had open-heart surgery for his congenital heart defect. Danny made it through the difficult surgery, but he developed complications. Shortly after coming out of anesthesia, he told his mother, "I don't want you to be afraid, Mom. I've seen an angel." He comforted his parents with this heavenly vision. He knew he was going to a better place. Danny never left the hospital.

French historian Philippe Aries, in his research, documented that even before A.D. 1000, "the dying would tell of visions of God and of seeing those who had died before them."[20]

It is my hope that people will come to accept *selected* predeath visions as blessings and real phenomena, not the curses or hallucinations they are often interpreted to be. Acceptance and understanding of these visions can transform fear and confusion into comfort and peace of mind. Hospice and other medical personnel can be instrumental in effecting these changes. Physicians are often in the best position to determine whether visions might be beneficial to reinforce. Dr. Morse described one such successful transition that he implemented:

It became clear that Mike wasn't afraid of the visions, just confused by them. In this stressful situation, Mike's parents were reacting to this confusion with fear of their own. Mike and I devised a plan. We developed cues that . . . gave Mike a feeling of mastery over the experiences. He began to relax and

interpret them for his family. His calm changed the
nature of these events for the family. Rather than
thinking he was delirious (which he wasn't), his
family was comforted by his visions. Instead of the
frightening episodes they once were, his parents
now wanted to know what he was seeing.[21]

Lastly, there was that *one* episode which had the greatest impact on *my* life, and this involved a colleague of
mine in the medical profession.

I remember walking into my office on a Monday morning and hearing that Tim, the son of a close friend and
colleague, had died the day before. I couldn't believe this.
Our own son had just played in a soccer game with him
yesterday. Unfortunately, it was quite true. Tim had been
with a group of boys, all on bicycles, a few hours after the
soccer game. At the same time, a next-door neighbor had
been inspecting the engine of his truck. When he was
finished, he slammed the hood closed. Immediately, the
truck lurched and began to roll backwards, down the
inclined street. Everything happened so fast. People
yelled down the street to get out of the way. Everyone
did—except Tim. John, his father, was one of the first on
the scene. Tim was fatally injured and probably died
instantly. John picked up his son and raced him in a car to
the hospital. All efforts proved futile. When I offered my
condolences to John and his family, his wife took me
aside and confided that John had been having recurrent
nightmares, involving Tim's death, for weeks preceding
his death. I was astounded! I tried immediately to reason
that "someone" had been trying to prepare John for this
ordeal. When John finally felt comfortable enough to relate the dream to me, it turned out the nightmare was
exceedingly accurate. His dream involved images of a
truck accident, John running down a street to the scene,
discovering and, in horror, picking up the limp body of

his son. Nonetheless, this story impacted me profoundly. John became suicidal for quite a time following this calamity. Despite at least one planned attempt to end his life, John ultimately decided against this drastic step. Perhaps the vision was the element that made the difference.

It was this incident which launched my intensive search into life's meaning, including the questions of justice and suffering. It is my duty as a physician to save lives. After studying NDEs, I questioned whether, perhaps, there might be instances in which we should *not* intervene. Even now, I still hold to the conviction that no one, including a doctor, should be an *active* participant in ending a life. However, I am convinced that *there are many times when physicians equally should not interfere with death*.

Up until now, I have not mentioned experiences of those who have attempted the ultimate interference with life—suicide. Moody observed several cases in which suicide appeared to have quite adverse ramifications:

> [While I was over there] I got the feeling that two things it would be completely forbidden for me to do would be to kill myself or to kill another person . . . If I were to commit suicide I would be throwing God's gift back in his face. . . Killing somebody else would be interfering with God's purpose for that individual.[22]

> Another man who survived an apparent clinical death of some duration said that while he was "over there," he had the impression that there was a "penalty" to pay for some acts of suicide, and that part of this would be to witness the suffering on the part of others that this act would cause.[23]

> One person . . . had the feeling that the state of

affairs in which she had been before her "death" was being repeated again and again, as if in a cycle.[24]

All mentioned that after their experiences, they would never consider trying suicide again.[25]

Others who experienced this unpleasant "limbo" state have remarked that they had the feeling they would be there for a long time. This was their penalty for "breaking the rules" by trying to release themselves prematurely from what was, in effect, an "assignment"—to fulfill a certain purpose in life.[26]

Hence, if the nature of the NDE signifies any preview at all of the next life, ending one's life may not represent the retreat from suffering that is hoped.

I will end this chapter with a Biblical narrative, which contains several elements of death-related visions. This is the story of the Apostle Paul's famous religious conversion on the road to Damascus. Note that, at this time in his life, Paul was an active persecutor of the Christians:

Thus I journeyed to Damascus with the authority and commission of the chief priests.

At midday, O king, I saw on the way a light from heaven, brighter than the sun, shining round me and those who journeyed with me.

And when we had all fallen to the ground, I heard a voice saying to me in the Hebrew language, "Saul, Saul, why do you persecute me? It hurts you to kick against the goads."

And I said, "Who are you, Lord?" And the Lord said, "I am Jesus whom you are persecuting.

But rise and stand upon your feet; for I have appeared to you for this purpose, to appoint you to serve and bear witness to the things in which you have seen me and to those in which I will appear to you, delivering you from the people and the Gentiles—to whom I send you to open their eyes, that they may turn from darkness to light and from the power of Satan to God, that they may receive forgiveness of sins and a place among those who are sanctified by faith in me."

Whereupon, O King Agrippa, I was not disobedient to the heavenly vision . . . Acts 26:12-19 (RSV)

This excerpt is noteworthy for the continued reference to "the light." As I will detail in the next chapter, this element of light is of exceptional importance.

# 2

# Light

$\mathbf{A}$s shown in the previous chapter, the element of light is one, if not *the*, most important element of the near-death experience. In reviewing multiple NDE cases, researchers Moody and Morse each made several note-worthy observations involving the light.

Moody noted that, of all the possible near-death elements, the light exerted the greatest influence on the individual. Patients interpreted the light as a being—a being who radiated love and warmth. Christians often recognized the light as Christ. Many atheists identified the spirit only as a guide. The entity communicated without words, by the "direct, unimpeded transfer of thoughts . . . , and in such a clear way that there [was] no possibility what-soever either of misunderstanding or of lying to the light."[1]

Morse documented similar descriptions of the light from his cases. Some identified the light as God, with the associated feelings of warmth, forgiveness, and unconditional love. The light embodied all truth and knowledge:[2]

> I have found the experience of light to be the keynote event of the near-death experience, the element that always leads to a transformation.[3]

The main question is: Why light? Why not darkness? Morse carefully analyzed this paradox. As blood flow to the brain ceases, our abilities for sight and comprehension fail. Tunnel vision ensues, and everything becomes dark. Physiologically, this is death. Yet, this is not what near-death victims see; they see light. There is no rational medical explanation for this occurrence.[4]

## The Nature of Light

A review of the true nature of light is necessary here before a discussion of its spiritual qualities. [Note: In this section, I will present a focused review of the behavior of waves and of scientific experiments involving light. Despite the detail provided, a complete understanding is not necessary to grasp the thesis I am constructing.]

Early in this century, research into the special attributes of light began. Scientists knew that electrons[5] interact by exchanging photons.[6] Moreover, if matter and antimatter chance to meet, the resulting annihilation ends in a flash of photons. The famous mathematician, Charles Hinton, believed that light was a "vibration of the fourth spatial dimension."[7] At about the same time, Albert Einstein was formulating his *special theory of relativity*, with its famous $E = mc^2$ [8] equation. Einstein made all previous notions of light obsolete.

Scientists know that light travels at 186,000 miles/second. In 1676, Danish astronomer Ole Rømer calculated the speed of light by measuring differences in timings between eclipses of Jupiter's moons. Rømer noted that the timings of the eclipses were different, depending on where the Earth lay in its annual orbit about the Sun. The eclipses were delayed when the Earth was on the far side of the Sun from Jupiter, compared to when it was on the near side. The delay was significant, more than a quarter of an hour, and the speed of light could be determined relatively easily.[9]

At the start of the twentieth century, physicists believed light proceeded by way of some unknown medium or "ether," similar to how sound waves, which cannot travel in a vacuum, propagate through air. Sound waves cannot travel in a vacuum. Let us compare the propagation of sound with light. If an observer travels in the same direction as a sound wave, it is possible to actually overtake the wave, as is seen when a jet airplane breaks the sound barrier. Sound waves travel at 1,088 feet/second. An onlooker traveling in the *same direction* as the sound wave, say at 200 ft./sec., would observe the speed of the sound wave to be 1,088 – 200, or 888 ft./sec. (**Figure 2.1**). Likewise, to an observer speeding along at 1,088 ft./sec., the observed speed of the wave would be zero.

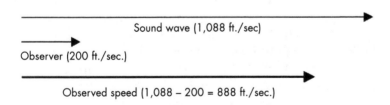

Sound wave (1,088 ft./sec)

Observer (200 ft./sec.)

Observed speed (1,088 – 200 = 888 ft./sec.)

**Figure 2.1 Relative Speed of Sound,
Travel in the Same Direction**

When traveling in the *opposite direction* at 200 ft./sec., the observed speed of the sound wave would increase by 200 ft./sec., or 1088 + 200 ft./sec. = 1288 ft./sec. (**Figure 2.2**). These are examples of classic Newtonian physics.

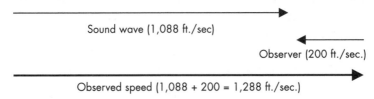

Sound wave (1,088 ft./sec)

Observer (200 ft./sec.)

Observed speed (1,088 + 200 = 1,288 ft./sec.)

**Figure 2.2 Relative Speed of Sound,
Travel in Opposite Direction**

When Einstein developed his special theory of relativity in 1905, the landscape of physics ideology was inexorably changed. As Einstein revealed, light *is* quite special and remarkable. Light does not require a medium in which to travel, and, unlike sound, its observed speed *never* changes, regardless of the *speed or direction* of the observer. A simple example will demonstrate this. An observer traveling beside a photon of light at, say, 100,000 miles/sec., would expect the *observed* speed of light to be 186,000 miles/sec. (the speed of light) - 100,000 miles/sec., or 86,000 miles/second. But contrary to what Newton would have reasoned, the special theory of relativity says the observed speed of the photon would be 186,000 miles/second—the same speed as if the observer were standing still (**Figure 2.3**).

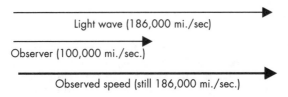

Light wave (186,000 mi./sec)

Observer (100,000 mi./sec.)

Observed speed (still 186,000 mi./sec.)

**Figure 2.3 Relative Speed of Light,
Travel in the Same Direction**

Einstein proposed that the speed of light is immutable. This was such a radical and unimaginable departure from then-current beliefs that, when Albert Michelson and E.W. Morley performed the now-famous series of experiments that reached the same conclusion in the 1880s, scientists regarded the results as erroneous and the experiments as failures.

Michelson conducted the first experiment while working in Berlin and, later, collaborated with Morley to im-

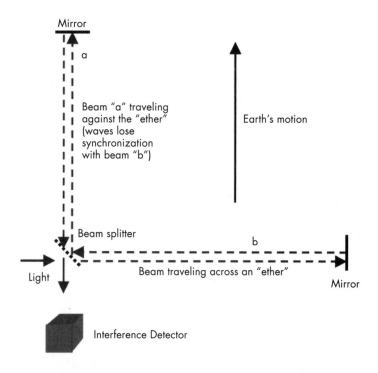

**Figure 2.4 Michelson-Morley Experiment.**[10] **Beam "a" traveling against an "ether" should slow in relation to beam "b." When the paths are reunited at the detector, the delayed waves of beam "a" should interfere with beam "b." Interference was not detected, proving the ether's absence.**

prove the methodology. The experiment utilized a semi-transparent mirror (not unlike mirrored sunglasses) to split a beam of light. The beam-splitter divided the two beams at a 90° angle. The researchers then reflected these divergent beams off distant mirrors and recombined them on their return, to determine any wave interference. Any observed interference would indicate the amount of slowing of one beam relative to the other (**Figure 2.4**). The team could then ascertain the velocity of each beam.[11] At this time, scientists believed an "ether" existed as the mysterious medium that permitted the transmission of light waves through space. Scientists expected the experiment to measure the speed of light at a slower velocity as it traveled *with* the Earth's motion and *against* the ether, than when moving *across* the ether. (I refer the reader to any introductory calculus text to verify that beam "a" would not catch up to beam "b" on its return

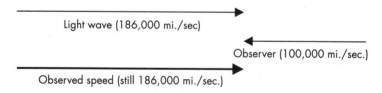

Light wave (186,000 mi./sec)

Observer (100,000 mi./sec.)

Observed speed (still 186,000 mi./sec.)

**Figure 2.5 Relative Speed of Light,
Travel in Opposing Direction**

leg.) Although the effects would be small, they would be measurable. As such, the waves of beam "a" should lose synchronization with beam "b," and interference would result when they were once again reunited. The results demonstrated conclusively that the speed of light was constant under both circumstances, refuting the presence of the ether.[12]

It is now universally accepted, although still incredible to comprehend, that the speed of light is constant for all observers, regardless of their relative speeds *or* direction. (**Figure 2.5**) This is an extraordinary feature.

How light accomplishes this feat is unknown, but it appears that light has been positioned as the cornerstone of modern physics and natural law. Einstein explained that, as an object increases in speed, especially approaching the speed of light, its length decreases, its mass increases, and time slows (but the speed of light remains constant). If an object actually *reaches* the speed of light, time stops completely. Many are not aware of the full significance of this last point. Imagine that you are traveling at the speed of light and time stands still. You find that you can travel anywhere in the universe and you never age! Hence, it is striking, but photons, and all other forms of electromagnetic radiation, are *timeless*. As astrophysicist John Gribbin summarized, an electromagnetic wave is "everywhere along its path (everywhere in the universe) at once; or you can say that distance does not exist for an electromagnetic wave."[13] Or, stated another way, "everything in the universe, past, present, and future, is connected to everything else, by a web of electromagnetic radiation that 'sees' everything at once."[14]

According to the special theory of relativity, nothing may *cross* the speed-of-light barrier. For practical purposes, this means that it is impossible to travel faster than the speed of light.[15] If this theoretical limitation is ever invalidated, it will open the door for the possibility of traveling backward in time.

What are the other ramifications for a form of energy that is timeless and travels? One not-so-evident answer is that light consists of *unlimited* energy. This infinite energy of the photon has resulted in perplexing problems for physicists. Electrons in atoms are constantly exchanging photons. Hence, when energy calculations of electrons and atoms were first being determined, the resulting sums were infinite.

Nobel prize-winning physicist Steven Weinberg demonstrated that such notable physicists as Werner Heisenberg, Wolfgang Pauli, and Ivar Waller were confronted by this problem. In 1930, Julius Robert Oppenheimer described the problem as being analogous to that of "a football quarterback catching his own forward pass." In all, since the energy of the photon is infinite, the resulting energy calculations of the atom are also infinite.[16]

Physicists currently resort to a controversial technique known as *renormalization* to eliminate the infinities from equations. This approach utilizes a method of cancellation of the infinities from both sides of an equation. Astrophysicist John Gribbin explained, "There is no legal mathematical way to get rid of the infinities, but it is possible to get rid of them by cheating . . . [T]he theorists remove the infinities from the equations, in effect dividing one infinity by another. Mathematically, if you divide infinity by infinity you could get any answer at all, and so they say that the answer must be . . . the measured mass of the electron."[17]

Steven Weinberg noted, "in order for the problem of infinities to be solved in this way, it is necessary that the infinities occur in calculations in only certain very limited ways, which is the case only for a limited class of specially simple quantum field theories. Such theories are called *renormalizable*. The simplest version of quantum electrodynamics is renormalizable in this sense, but any sort of small change in this theory . . . would lead not only to a disagreement with experiment but to results that were totally absurd—infinite answers to perfectly sensible questions."[18]

Paul Davies described his attitude toward the renormalization methodology this way: "Whenever the quantum theory of fields was applied to all but the simplest processes, the answers always turned out to be infinite . . . In the case of the electromagnetic field, a subtle mathematical sleight-of-hand enabled the infinities to be side-stepped . . ."[19]

Even renowned physicist Stephen Hawking is not at ease with the technique. He stated, "Rather similar, seemingly absurd infinities occur in the other partial theories, but in all these cases the infinities can be cancelled out by a process called renormalization. This involves cancelling the infinities by introducing other infinities. Although this technique is rather dubious mathematically, it does seem to work in practice, and has been used with these theories to make predictions that agree with observations to an extraordinary degree of accuracy. Renormalization, however, does have a serious drawback from the point of view of trying to find a complete theory, because it means that the actual values of the masses and the strengths of the forces cannot be predicted from the theory, but have to be chosen to fit the observations."[20]

So, at least for the present, physicists have found a means to deal with infinities, and, at the same time, have admitted that the infinite energy of light is real. This attribute of light is especially meaningful. Amit Goswami, Ph.D., author and professor of physics at the University of Oregon, concluded, "Light is the only reality."[21] George Johnson concurred: "Einstein taught us that light reigns supreme."[22] Physicist and author Gerald Schroeder even goes so far as to make a comparison between light and God, noting that both exist outside of time: "Einstein showed us, in the flow of light, the corollary of the Eternal Now: I was, I am, I will be."[23] Today, more scientists recognize the significance of electromagnetic radiation, which pervades our daily lives, even to the point of being compared to God. If a relationship possibly exists between light and a Supreme Being, perhaps it manifests in other ways. Incredibly, physicists have performed experiments that suggest light is conscious!

## The Double-Slit Experiment

One of the properties of waves is the phenomenon of *diffraction*. Diffraction is defined as the bending of a wave into the region behind an obstacle. If a wave encounters a small opening in a wall, equal to or smaller than its wavelength (a wavelength is the distance between two consecutive wave crests or two consecutive wave troughs),

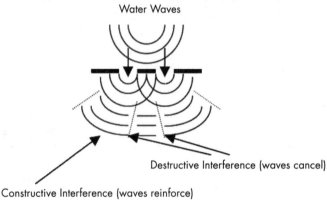

Water Waves

Destructive Interference (waves cancel)

Constructive Interference (waves reinforce)

**Figure 2.6 Interference of Water Waves**

the wave propagates beyond the opening as a semicircle. We have all witnessed this event with water waves. If the waves encounter *two* holes in the wall, instead of one, the resulting semicircles from each opening will *interfere* with one another (**Figure 2.6**). At some places the crests from two waves will coincide, producing a relatively high wave (*constructive interference*). At other locations, a crest and a trough will coincide and cancel each other out (*destructive interference*). All waves display the property of interference, and light is no exception.

However, in 1905, Einstein demonstrated that light had properties characteristic of particles as well as waves, a discovery (the photoelectric effect) for which he later received the Nobel Prize. Since that time, this dual nature, inherent in light, has become known as the "wave-particle duality." A *single photon* is defined as a discrete unit of electromagnetic radiation, and, as such, may be identified as either a particle or wave, or both. Hence, for the remainder of this book, the reader will find that there is little distinction made between a light wave and a light particle. (By the end of the book, I hope to convince you of the ill-defined nature of *any* particle and wave.)

In 1803, Thomas Young conducted the first double-slit experiment using light (**Figure 2.7**). He demonstrated that light, passing through a single, narrow slit (equal to or less than the wavelength of visible light) creates a

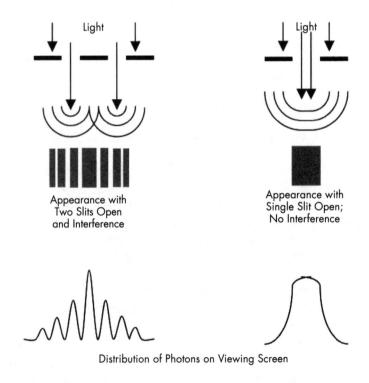

Appearance with
Two Slits Open
and Interference

Appearance with
Single Slit Open;
No Interference

Distribution of Photons on Viewing Screen

**Figure 2.7 The Double-Slit Experiment[24]**

narrow, fuzzy image on the screen. The fuzziness is the result of the diffraction of light. If there are two narrow slits, the light produces an interference pattern of alternating light and dark bands (instead of just two fuzzy, light bands).

Now for the *coup de grace*. What might one expect if, in the above experiment, the photons are fired through the slits *one at a time*? An educated person might expect that there would be no interference, as it would be unlikely that a *single photon* could travel through both slits simultaneously and then *interfere with itself*. Nonetheless, this is exactly what apparently happens. As each sequential photon appears on the screen (or photographic plate), one would reasonably expect two light bands to emerge. Instead, the typical interference pattern of multiple, alternating, light and dark bands forms. Thus, **Figure 2.7** is equally accurate for photons that are fired one at a time. This is the enigma of the double-slit experiment. As each successive photon is fired, its appearance on the screen falls *only* in the bands of the interference pattern if *both* slits are open, and *only* in the single region if a *single* slit is open. The far-reaching conclusion of this experiment is that *some form of communication* is occurring *within* the light wave, informing it where it is, or is not, appropriate to land on the screen. Several renowned authors and physicists have reached the same verdict:

Even if the photon is infinitely extended, in the time it travels from the photon gun to the open slit, it cannot have "felt" the second slit, checked to see if that second slit was open or closed, communicated that information to the portion passing through the first slit and then decided where on the screen it was permitted to land and where it was forbidden . . .

This is bizarre. With only one slit open, the particle could land anywhere within the fuzzy region

marked on the screen . . . With two slits open, this is
no longer true . . . There are forbidden regions, the
dark bands [In Figure 2.7, the white gaps of the
black-striped interference pattern represent these
'dark' bands].[25] (Gerald Schroeder)

When we fired our photon and it went through
the first slit, how did it "know" that it could go to an
area that must be dark if the other slit were open? In
other words, how did the photon know that the
other slit was closed? . . .
There is no definitive answer to this question.
Some physicists, like E.H. Walker, speculate that
photons may be conscious! . . .
We have little choice but to acknowledge that photons, which are energy, do appear to process information and to act accordingly.[26] (Gary Zukav)

John Gribbin, Ph.D., an astrophysicist from Cambridge
University, made his point by including a reference by
physicist and Nobel Prize winner Richard Feynman:

The basic element of quantum theory, says
Feynman on page 1 of the volume on his *Lectures*
devoted to quantum mechanics, is the double-slit
experiment. Why? Because this is "a phenomenon
which is impossible, *absolutely* impossible, to explain
in any classical way . . . In reality, it contains the *only*
mystery . . . the basic peculiarities of all quantum
mechanics."[27]

If this ability of light to "communicate" seems fantastic,
consider that the same has been found true of *electrons,
protons*, and even *entire atoms* when they were fired through
openings in identical experiments. This observation lends
credence to the possibility that all matter, which is just

another form of energy, may exhibit this "consciousness." For those who might wonder if this observed peculiarity of light is unique to the double-slit experiment, similar experiments have reached the same remarkable conclusion:

- **The calcite crystal experiment.** Calcite has the property of being able to split light into two beams. In this experiment, researchers used calcite, instead of two slits, to divide the light. Again, a *single photon* of light was proven to apparently split in two and follow both paths in the experiment *when both paths are open*. With *only one path unobstructed*, the "intact" photon chose either the closed or open passage, and was, hence, observed to complete the *open* circuit only 50 percent of the time (as opposed to "half" the photon completing the open circuit 100 percent of the time). Again, the photon appeared to be "aware whether or not the other channel has been blocked off, and has modified its behavior accordingly. All of this is old hat, by the standards of quantum theory, and has been known for decades."[28] (John Gribbin)

- **The delayed choice experiment.** This experiment was unusual, in that the experimenter decided whether a device would interfere in the final light pathway, during the last picosecond ($10^{-12}$ second) of the test. The results of this test indicated that the "photons seem to respond even to our delayed choice instantly and retroactively. A photon travels one path or both paths, exactly in harmony with our choice. How does it know?"[29] (Amit Goswami)

- **The quantum eraser experiment.** This clever 1991 experiment by physicist Martin Scully again utilized the crystal's property to split single photons. Each resultant half was directed (via mirrors) to a beam splitter (a *semitransparent* mirror that ei-

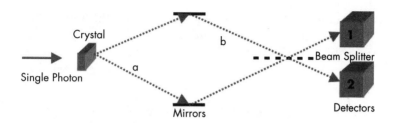

**Figure 2.8 Quantum Eraser Experiment, Possible Paths**[31]

ther transmitted or reflected light 50:50 percent of the time). **Figure 2.8** displays the different *possible* pathways available to the photons.[30]

The photons were seen to travel in the above manner to either Detector 1 or 2, but never to both simultaneously. They appeared to reconstruct themselves into the photon's original configuration, whereby, if one half was *reflected* at the beam splitter, the other half was always *transmitted* **(Figure 2.9)**.

The experimenters then modified the investigation by placing a 90° polarizer in pathway "a." This alteration permitted researchers to identify the "a"

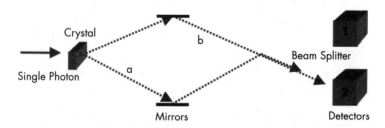

**Figure 2.9 Quantum Eraser Experiment, Actual Paths (Both half beams unite to travel to either Detector 1 or 2, but never both simultaneously.)**[32]

photon. Inexplicably, this "monitoring" tactic (to be discussed in Chapter 4) altered the reconstructive mechanism as seen in **Figure 2.9**. The photons then traveled both final pathways, *triggering both detectors simultaneously* (**Figure 2.10**).

The final modification was the addition of "reversing" polarizers (to reverse the effect of polarizer P) positioned in front of the detectors (**Figure 2.11**).

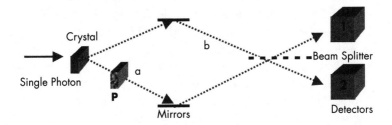

**Figure 2.10 Quantum Eraser Experiment, with Polarizer (P)[33]**

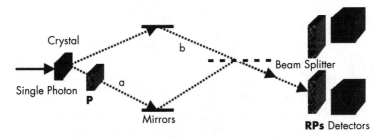

**Figure 2.11 Quantum Eraser Experiment, with Reversing Polarizers (RPs)[34]**

The reversing polarizers, by negating the effect of polarizer P, once again allow the photons to reconstruct into their original configurations (i.e., triggering either detector 1 or 2, but not both simultaneously). The special significance of this last adjustment is the change provoked by the set of reversing polarizers— *a change that was transmitted retroactively, after* the photons had traversed the circuit.[35]

Certainly, even if light does not possess a conscious-ness as we know it, it appears to exhibit an acute aware-ness of its surroundings and reacts accordingly. In doing so, it proves that this comprehension is instantaneous; i.e., faster than the speed of light. This trait will be dis-cussed in greater depth in later chapters. For now, we view the first hint of its existence in the double-slit ex-periment, whereby we witness that *light has an immediate knowledge of its surrounding environment and acts accord-ingly.*

Niels Bohr, Danish physicist and Nobel Prize winner, summarized it best when he said, *"Those who are not shocked when they first come across quantum theory cannot possibly have understood it."*[36]

## Similarities to God

The above research raises the following question: Is there any evidence of a direct link between light and a Supreme Designer of the universe? The answer is "Yes." Although many feel that God manifests Him/Herself through all of nature, there seems to be a special relation-ship to light, as witnessed throughout the whole of his-tory. Let's review the facts, up to this point:

1. Light represents the cornerstone to the special theory of relativity and all modern physics.
2. Both electromagnetic radiation (including light) and God exist outside of time.
3. Light is one of the major features of the near-death

experience, apparently our closest preview of what may await us beyond death.

4. Light exhibits an uncanny and unexplained awareness, or consciousness, of its surroundings.

5. This awareness, on light's part, occurs instantaneously and, hence, faster than the speed of light.

Other close relationships also link these two entities. One of the first findings is that light made up one of the major forces present at the formation of the universe; i.e., the Big Bang. Likewise, at the very end, light will equally predominate. If the universe ultimately contracts (the Big Crunch), it will result in a fiery collapse, manifesting largely as light. Conversely, if the death of the universe occurs as the result of continued expansion (as opposed to contraction), then the future foresees "a dismal fate for the universe . . . populated at an ever-decreasing density by a few isolated neutrinos and photons, and very little else"[37] (Paul Davies). It is intriguing to realize the perseverance of light, one of the first, as well as one of the last, features of the known universe—the alpha and the omega? Of course, this is purely circumstantial evidence of a possible relationship, but is, nonetheless, fascinating.

Lastly, there are the countless references to light in the world's major religious texts. One source[38] lists sixty-one such references in the Bible (thirty-six Old Testament, twenty-five New Testament). Similar references appear in the Apocrypha, Kabbalah, Book of Mormon, Koran, and Bhagavad Gita. Pertinent excerpts, such as the following examples, are plentiful:

Bless the Lord, O my soul!
O Lord my God, thou art very great!
Thou art clothed with honor and majesty,
who coverest thyself with *light* as with a garment . . .
Psalms 104:1-2 (RSV)

He came for testimony, to bear witness to the *light*,
that all might believe through him. John 1:7

Again Jesus spoke to them, saying, "I am the *light*
of the world; he who follows me will not walk in
darkness, but will have the *light* of life." John 8:12

'I send you to open their eyes, that they may turn
from darkness to *light*, and from the power of Satan
to God . . .' Acts 26:17-18

[Y]ou may declare the wonderful deeds of him
who called you out of darkness into his marvelous
*light*. I Peter 2:9

This is the message we have heard from him and
proclaim to you, that God is *light* and in him is no
darkness at all. I John 1:5

And the city has no need of sun or moon to shine
upon it, for the glory of God is its *light*, and its lamp
is the Lamb. Revelation 21:23

For she [wisdom] is a reflection of the everlasting
*light*,
And a spotless mirror of the activity of God
Apocrypha: The Wisdom of Solomon 7:26[39]

For God will lead Israel with joy, by the *light* of his
glory. Apocrypha: The Book of Baruch 5:9[40]

The *light* created by God in the act of Creation
flared from one end of the universe to the other
and was hidden away,
reserved for the righteous in the world that is
coming,

as it is written:
'*Light* is sown for the righteous.' . . .
Since the first day, the *light* has never been fully revealed,
but it is vital to the world,
renewing each day the act of Creation. Kabbalah, "Creation"[41]

So if you pray and offer a blessing to God, or if you wish your intention to be true, imagine that you are *light*. All around you—in every corner and on every side—is *light*. Turn to your right, and you will find shining *light*; to your left, splendor, a radiant *light*. Between them, up above, the *light* of the Presence. Surrounding that, the *light* of life. Above it all, a crown of *light* . . . This *light* is unfathomable and endless. Kabbalah, "Mind, Meditation, and Mystical Experience"[42]

Christ] is the *light* and life of the world; yea, a *light* that is endless, that can never be darkened; yea, and also a life which is endless, that there can be no more death. Book of Mormon: Mosiah 16:9[43]

[Ye] should search diligently in the *light* of Christ that ye may know good from evil . . . Book of Mormon: Moroni 7:19[44]

God is the *light* of the heavens and the earth. His *light* may be compared to a niche that enshrines a lamp, the lamp within a crystal of star-like brilliance. It is lit from a blessed olive tree neither eastern nor western. Its very oil would almost shine forth, though no fire touched it. *Light* upon *light*; God guides to His *light* whom He will. Koran 24:35[45]

They seek to extinguish the *light* of God with their mouths; but God will perfect His *light*, much as the unbelievers may dislike it. Koran 61:8[46]

Of a thousand suns in the sky
If suddenly should burst forth
The *light*, it would be like
Unto the *light* of that exalted one.
Bhagavad Gita: XI:12[47]

A mass of radiance, glowing on all sides,
I see Thee, hard to look at, on every side
With the glory of flaming fire and sun, immeasurable.
Bhagavad Gita: XI:17[48]

In these passages, it is clear that the "light" is referring
to God or, for Christians, often to the Christ. Several of
the above excerpts, in addition, refer to the darkness—or
Satan. Unquestionably, the story of Satan plays a major
role in the history of the human race.

Bestselling author and psychiatrist Scott Peck reviewed
Lucifer's former background as instructor and "light
bearer."[49] The devil rose up against God and was cast into
Hell. At the end of time, one of two possible outcomes is
predicted for Satan: 1) It eventually converts to the side
of good, or 2) it maintains its evil convictions, refusing
ever to give in to overtures for forgiveness.[50]

Lucifer has earned for itself a relegated position over
darkness. In contrast, light has always represented right-
eousness, God, or Christ. As noted in near-death experiences, the light is also associated with intense feelings of
peace and love. A characteristic account by a cardiac arrest victim closes this chapter:

[T]here was this bright light. It got brighter and
brighter. And I seemed to go through it.
All of a sudden I was just somewhere else. There
was a gold-looking light, everywhere. Beautiful. I

couldn't find a source anywhere. It was just all around, coming from everywhere. There was music. And I seemed to be in a countryside with streams, grass, and trees, mountains. But when I looked around—if you want to put it that way—they were not trees and things like we know them to be . . .

There was a sense of perfect peace and contentment; love. It was like I was part of it.[51] (Moody)

# 3

# Faster than a Speeding Bullet

We discussed light waves, noting that they are apparently aware of their surroundings and able to act accordingly. We also reviewed the behavior of photons, which apparently are able to communicate this behavior instantaneously at the speed of light. There are several theories that attempt to explain this phenomenon. John Cramer advanced one such theory in an article in the *Reviews of Modern Physics*,[1] in 1986. In this article, he suggested that this observed form of communication is achieved by an "offer wave," which is extended into the future. This wave is then returned in the form of a "confirmation wave," which travels backward in time, containing the necessary information for the entity (photon, electron, etc.) to adjust to its surroundings. Cramer termed this transaction "a 'handshake' across space-time."[2] The only aberration in this hypothesis is the proposition that the "offer and confirmation waves" perform their combined travel and function *atemporally*; i.e., instantaneously or outside of time. Since no wave, so far as we know, can travel faster than the speed of light, these cannot be waves in the traditional sense, and, as such, many physicists prefer the word "influence" instead of wave. Waves, such as electromagnetic and light waves, are limited to the speed of light (consider, for example, cellular phone signals). They are called *local*. The remaining influences, which act atemporally, traveling faster than the speed of light, are called *nonlocal* (no common examples—perhaps, visions and telepathy). However, despite its esoteric nature, physicists and mathematicians have actually proven nonlocality.

## The EPR Experiment and Bell's Inequality

In the 1930s, Einstein, Boris Podolsky and Nathan Rosen (EPR) collaborated in a thought experiment, which is now known as the EPR experiment. These men conceived this experiment as *an argument against nonlocality*. Einstein had always been an outspoken opponent of this concept, as he believed it implied "that reality is observer-created."[3] (This "power of observation" will be discussed at length in the next chapter.) Einstein did not live to see the experiment performed, however. In 1964, John Bell published the first *mathematical* proof[4] (called Bell's theorem or Bell's inequality) verifying nonlocality. It was not until 1972, that John Clauser, a Ph.D. from Columbia University, conducted the actual *scientific* EPR experiment at Berkeley. In 1982, Alain Aspect, a physicist at the University of Paris, repeated an enhanced version of the experiment. Both experiments verified nonlocality.[5] To understand the EPR experiments, I have adapted a lengthy, but necessary, description by Nick Herbert.[6] The following explanation simplifies the most difficult concept of this book, essentially revealing that one plus one does not equal two.

In the experiment, a stimulated particle (an atom) produces two photons, each traveling in opposite directions. For example, when electrically excited, the atoms of some elements, such as mercury or calcium, produce pairs of photons in this manner. As the photons from each pair separate, they are observed to be identical in all respects, including one important quality (for the purpose of this EPR experiment) known as *polarization*. Polarization is the angle at which the lightwave is oriented in space (see **Figure 3.1**). Understanding the definition is not as important as understanding that the two photons are indistinguishable, except for their direction of travel. Thus, if one is polarized vertically at 0°, so is the other. If one is oriented horizontally at 90°, then, so is the other. Clauser and Aspect utilized this basis to conduct their investigations of nonlocality.

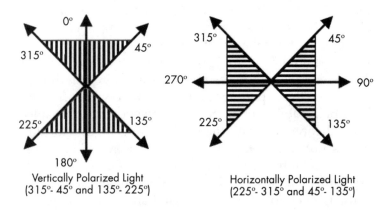

Vertically Polarized Light
(315°- 45° and 135°- 225°)

Horizontally Polarized Light
(225°- 315° and 45°- 135°)

**Figure 3.1 Vertically and Horizontally Polarized Light**

A calcite detector is an instrument used to measure the polarity of photons. This state-of-the-art device determines whether a light wave is oriented *vertically* (designated by **V**) or *horizontally* (**H**).[7] In the laboratory, to identify the polarities of two photons, each traveling in opposite directions, two detectors (**A** and **B**) are used, one each at opposite ends of the laboratory. Similarly, investigators could just as well place the detectors on Earth and a distant star. If each calcite detector yields the *same readings as its opposite,* the "error rate" is said to be zero, as illustrated by **Figure 3.2**:

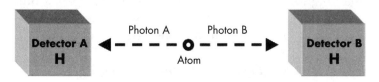

Detector A: VVHHHVVHHHHHVVVHVVHHH
Detector B: VVHHHVVHHHHHVVVHVVHHH

**Figure 3.2 Error Rate of Zero (The readings are identical.)[8]**

Unfortunately, no matter how good the measuring device, there will be errors. For instance, photons that are oriented at 45° (halfway between 0° and 90°) might be measured as either V or H,[9] resulting in mismatches **(Figure 3.3)**:

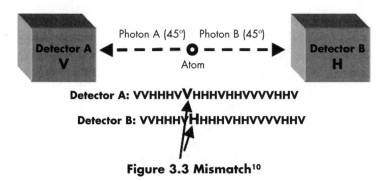

Detector A: VVHHHV**V**HHHHVHHVVVVHHV

Detector B: VVHHHV**H**HHHVHHVVVVHHV

**Figure 3.3 Mismatch[10]**

Good investigators always consider the potential error rates in their experiments, and these scientists did as well. Clauser and Aspect each calculated the error rate and found that accounting for the mismatches actually supported their conclusions. I will explain.

Since this investigation involves the measurement of angles (i.e., light's polarization angle), physicists correctly anticipated that turning or changing the angle of either or both detectors would alter the results. For instance, altering the angle of **Detector A** by 45° would throw its readings off by 45°. Light originally oriented at 45° is now unambiguously measured as 0° or V (45° - 45° = 0°). Moreover, light initially oriented at 70° (which would previously have been measured as horizontal [closer to 90° than 0°]) is now read as vertical (70° - 45° = 25°), since it is now nearer 0° (**Figures 3.4 and 3.5**). Suffice it to say, changing the angle of the detector modified its readings.

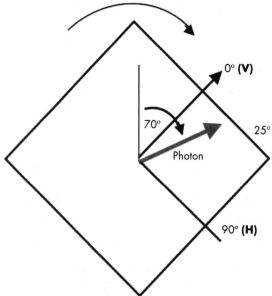

**Figure 3.4 If the detector is rotated 45°, a 70° polarized photon is "read" as V (70°- 45° = 25°) instead of H.**

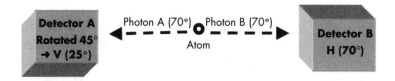

**Figure 3.5 Rotating Detector A Changes Its Readings.**

Furthermore, it was assumed that changing the angle of *only* **Detector A** would change *only* **A**'s results. Similarly, changing the angle of *only* **Detector B** would change *only* **B**'s results. As an illustration, let's say **Detector A** is rotated 22.5° (half of 45°), and there is a resultant error rate (or mismatch) of 1:4 (**Figure 3.6**).

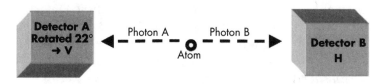

Detector A: **V**VH**H**HV**V**HHHV**H**H**V**VV**H**H**H
Detector B: **H**VHHHV**H**HHHV**V**H**H**VVV**H**H**V**

**Figure 3.6 Errors are 1:4 with Detector A Rotated 22.5° (half of 45°)[11]**

If **Detector B** is now *also* rotated 22.5 degrees, but in the opposite direction, the detectors are now misaligned by a **total of 45° degrees**. The **error rate** would be expected to be **twice as much, or 2:4.** (For those of you who are presently overwhelmed, you may skip immediately to the following paragraph without missing any critical information.) Yet, wait—we have failed to consider that some errors by **Detector A** may occasionally cancel out the errors of **Detector B**, and vice versa. For instance, a V/H mismatch, caused by rotating **Detector A**, now changes to V/V by rotating *also* **Detector B**. Hence, an occasional mismatch will inevitably be changed back to a match. As such, the *error rate cannot be greater than twice that observed by rotating only one detector, or no more than 2:4.*

So, what is the actual result? The mathematical proof by Bell *and* the scientific experiments by Clauser and Aspect (using the detectors) revealed *an error rate of 3:4!* What was especially interesting about the Clauser experiment is that Clauser performed his investigation in an effort to *disprove* Bell's proof. Instead, he ended up verifying it!

What is the conclusion to these complex experiments? The results indicate that *rotating Detector A, say, on Earth, also alters the results of measurements by Detector B, on a distant star.* These changes occur *without rotating* **Detector B** (Note: The added rotation of **Detector B** in the above experiment was required only for the *detection* of the change.). These results indicate that *our actions on Earth are causing changes in other parts of the universe.* Recall that a local signal (or "locality," as physicists like to call it) is limited to the speed of light. *These experiments prove that particle/wave communication occurs nonlocally and faster than the speed of light.* Keep in mind, the specific moving particle or wave remains restricted to the speed of light. Only its *ability to communicate* occurs instantaneously.

Physicists believe that the explanation behind this quantum phenomenon lies in the inherent link of all matter to the Big Bang, called *phase entanglement.* American physicist Nick Herbert (who coined the term *quon* to be "any entity . . . that exhibits both wave and particle aspects in the peculiar quantum manner"[12]) gave the following analysis:

> Phase entanglement . . . instantly connects any two quons which have once interacted . . . Since

there is nothing that is not ultimately a quantum system, if the quantum phase connection is "real," then it links all systems that have once interacted at some time in the past—not just twin-state photons—into a single waveform whose remotest parts are joined in a manner unmediated, unmitigated, and immediate . . . What phase entanglement really is we may never know, but Bell's theorem tells us that it is no limp mathematical fiction but a reality to be reckoned with.[13]

In his celebrated theorem, Bell did not merely suggest or hint that reality is nonlocal, he actually proved it, invoking the clarity and power of mathematical reasoning.[14]

Instantaneous communication is considered a genuine, quantum fact and an element of day-to-day reality. Could these phenomena of phase entanglement and superluminal (faster than the speed of light) communication have any connections to the previously discussed *visions of knowledge* of near-death experiences? Let us assume, for the time being, that NDEs are real phenomena. During these occurrences, the victim departs the physical body (with instantaneous, unlimited travel), and interacts (including communication) with the *Light* (experiencing warmth, peace, love, and enlightenment). Released from the restrictions of time, this spirit (soul) can be everywhere at once, in touch with all past, present, and future events (and, hence, all knowledge), immersed in the grandeur of immediate interaction with the entire universe. Remember that the universe includes all energy forms such as light and radiation, as well as matter ($E = mc^2$). This universal connectivity could well explain the omniscience described in these out-of-body adventures. Similarly, this knowledge would vanish upon return of the soul back to the body, as it relinquishes its bond to the Light, just as these examples illustrate:

> Several people have told me that during their encounters with "death," they got brief glimpses of an entire separate realm of existence in which all knowledge—whether of past, present, or future—seemed to co-exist in a sort of timeless state. Alternately, this has been described as a moment of enlightenment in which the subject seemed to have complete knowledge. In trying to talk about this aspect of their experience, all have commented that this experience was ultimately inexpressible. Also, all agree that this feeling of complete knowledge did not persist after their return . . .[15] (Moody)

> It seemed that all of a sudden, all knowledge—of all that had started from the very beginning, that would go on without end—that for a second I knew all the secrets of all the ages, all the meaning of the universe, the stars, the moon—of everything. But after I chose to return, this knowledge escaped, and I can't remember any of it.[16] (Moody)

> Knowledge and information are readily available—all knowledge . . . You absorb knowledge . . . You all of a sudden know the answers.[17] (Moody)

> Then, for an instant, it seemed as if I knew everything, that everything made sense. Suddenly, I intuitively understood math and science, and I don't know beans about math and science.[18] (Sharp)

Similarly, there is no reason that superluminal communication could not be used to explain a number of other previously unexplained phenomena, including telepathy and the collective unconscious (to be discussed), as well as certain aspects of the near-death and death-related experiences.

Consider Gary Zukav's observation:

> Superluminal quantum connectedness seems to be, on the surface at least, a possible explanation for some types of psychic phenomena. Telepathy, for example, often appears to happen instantaneously, if not faster. Psychic phenomena have been held in disdain by physicists since the days of Newton. In fact, most physicists do not even believe that they exist.
>
> In this sense, Bell's theorem could be the Trojan horse in the physicists' camp; first, because it proves that quantum theory requires connections that appear to resemble telepathic communication, and second, because it provides the mathematical framework through which serious physicists (all physicists are serious) could find themselves discussing types of phenomena which, ironically, they do not believe exist.[19]

## The Beginning

To understand the intimate link of all matter in the universe, it would be worthwhile to review several aspects of the event that sparked our universe, the Big Bang. Most cosmologists believe the universe is the result of a "quantum fluctuation" or vacillation in the pre-Big Bang environment. That is to say, the universe formed from nothing. We know that the vacuum of space is not a pure vacuum, that it is actually seething with activity. Stephen Hawking noted, "The trouble is . . . that even 'empty' space is filled with pairs of virtual particles and their antiparticles. These pairs would have an infinite amount of energy and, therefore, by Einstein's famous equation $E = mc^2$, they would have an infinite amount of mass."[20]

As these electron-positron pairs materialize from the vacuum, they "quickly annihilate one other and give their borrowed energy back to the vacuum" (Gribbin).[21] Likewise, as other forms of energy and matter emerge from the vacuum, the length of their existence is constrained by their mass. Hence, a photon of light (having zero rest mass) would linger longer than a more massive electron-positron pair.[22]

In summary, particles of infinite energies may arise from quantum fluctuations, despite the limitation of their survival by their mass. However, *gravity* is known to exhibit *negative* energy and could exactly counterbalance the positive energy of mass. It is from such evidence that physicists postulate that the Big Bang occurred. Keep in mind the inconsistency that an active vacuum was *unlikely to have existed prior to the Big Bang!* Despite this drawback, the Big Bang theory is still highly regarded, and represents the best *scientific* hypothesis for the creation of the universe:

> There is almost unanimous opinion among scientists that the entire cosmos originated between ten and twenty billion years ago in a big bang, and that this event set the universe on the road to its ultimate destiny.[23] (Davies)

Thus, the universe came into being, an unfathomable blast of a singularity[24] from the void. As such, the present universe has evolved, not unlike the surface of a growing sphere, ever expanding through space-time, the result of this grand miracle. It is this past inherent association of all current matter, light, and energy to the Big Bang that permits the wonders of phase entanglement and superluminal communication.

# 4

# Beyond Observation

If you believe concepts introduced in previous chapters were extraordinary, then the principles discussed in this chapter will equally test your rationality.

Before we examine the next set of experiments, it is useful to understand how single photons are produced. To create a single photon,[1] physicists direct a laser of just the proper intensity at calcium atoms. When a photon (e.g., from the laser) strikes an electron orbiting the atom, the resultant, stimulated electron springs from its ground orbital level to a higher energy level. In this new location, the electron is highly unstable and will quickly return to its stable ground state. As the electron makes the transition back to this lower level, it releases an individual photon. Consequently, these individual photons can be directed at specified targets for experimentation.

In the double-slit experiment (Chapter 2), single photons exhibited the unusual trait of *surrounding-awareness*, or, as some have said, *consciousness*. Investigators arranged for these photons to pass, one at a time, through the slits. We know from the earlier experiments described that, without a detector, a typical interference pattern appears (alternating light and dark bands), as illustrated in **Figure 4.1A**. The slits caused the single light wave to split in two. Each half traveled through each slit, and the halves then converged, producing the interference pattern.

With only one slit, no interference pattern developed (**Figure 4.1B**).

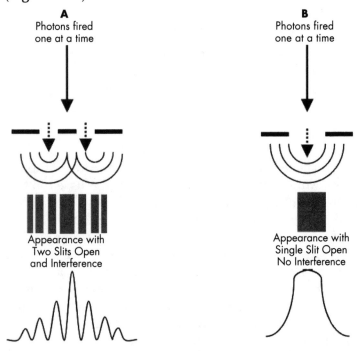

Distribution of Photons on Viewing Screen[2]

**Figure 4.1 Photons Fired One at a Time.**

In a further modification of the double-slit experiment, researchers placed a photon detector at only *one* of the two slits. No device monitored the second slit. With a particle detector positioned at one of the slits, physicists again directed the photons, one at a time, toward the two slits. An unexpected, two-band pattern emerged (**Figure 4.2**). The individual photons *no longer* split in two, i.e., traveling through both slits at the same time. Instead,

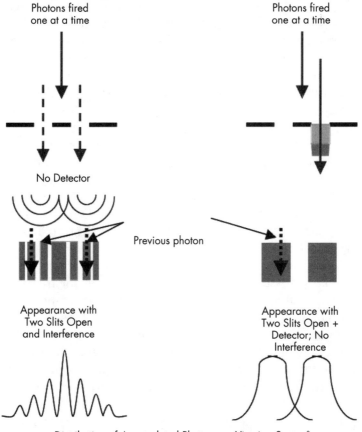

Distribution of Accumulated Photons on Viewing Screen[3]

**Figure 4.2 Modified Double-Slit Experiment**

each photon apparently sensed the presence of the detector, and traveled as a whole particle through one slit or the other, but not both at the same time. As each successive light wave was fired, the dots accumulated on the photographic plate to reveal only two bands. The light wave was, once again, reacting to its surroundings, i.e., the presence of the detector, and acting accordingly.

In the realm of classical physics, the conditions of two situations illustrated in **Figure 4.2** are identical. The presence of the detector should not alter the outcome. The detector is purely an observation device. Still, the photon perceived the detector and, as a result, remained whole. Not only did the photon *fail to split in two,* but it ventured into areas where it would not in the detector's absence. The reverse was also true: Without the detector, the photon split in two, and materialized (with the interference pattern) in areas that it would not in the detector's presence; i.e., the two-band pattern. [In a similar situation, you may recall that "labeling" the split photons with a polarizer in the quantum eraser experiment (**Figure 2.10**) also induced modifications to the photon's path, which then disappeared with insertion of reversing polarizers **(Figure 2.11).**]

Why the presence of the monitors should cause such alterations is unknown. There is no reason for the photons to materialize into one pattern in one instance, and then materialize into a different pattern under seemingly analogous circumstances (with only the addition of a detecting device). What forces are at play, making the photon react *prior* to reaching the detector? Consider that the photon had made its choice on whether to split into two *before* it even reached the slits and the detector. The photon chose to split into two before reaching the slits when no detector was present, and to remain whole when a detector sat on the other side.

Gerald Schroeder emphasized that the results indicate

"the end of the line for causality."[4] Identical conditions should give identical results. This set of experiments indicated otherwise. One possible implication is that the act of observation is altering the light. Another is that the light is reacting to the monitor. Or both. Either way, we are now aware of new capabilities for light and the act of observation.

This *awareness by light* is not peculiar to forms of electromagnetic radiation, but extends to other particles and, conceivably, to any material object. For instance, if electrons are employed instead of photons, the results are identical. A "particle" acts as a wave in the absence of an observation device, but travels as an intact particle when a detector is present. Some scientists maintain that the universe exists primarily as waves, coalescing into particles *only under the act of observation:*

> What you find in such a situation [with a detector in place] is that each electron is always seen to be a particle, travelling through one hole or the other. It behaves like a little bullet. And, lo and behold, the interference pattern disappears. Instead, the pattern on the screen becomes the pattern produced by little bullets travelling through each hole independently (or by rocks thrown through two holes in a wall). The act of observing the electron wave makes it collapse and behave like a particle at the crucial moment when it is going through the hole.[5] (Gribbin)

Physicists have coined the phrase "collapse of the wave function" to describe this transformation of wave into particle. An important difference between a wave and a particle is that a wave is capable of splitting into two halves; a particle cannot.

We find that whether a single detector, at only *one* of the two slits, or a detector at *each* slit is employed, the outcome remains the same. *It is the presence of any detector,* not the number, which causes the wave's conversion to a particle.

Consider also that, until recently, photon detectors had only about 10 percent efficiency.[6] As such, for every ten photons that passed through a detector, only one was actually measured. In the double-slit experiment, why did the interference pattern not emerge as a result of the nine (out of ten) photons that were not detected? At the very least, a mixed pattern (of interference overlying the two-band pattern) should have appeared. This was not the case. The detector's presence collapsed *all* the light waves, not just the one-out-of-ten being measured.

The resulting deduction is that *the fact of observation profoundly altered the outcome* of the double-slit experiment. Light remains as a wave without observation, but coalesces to a particle when scrutinized.

An equally dramatic experiment supports the same conclusion. Researchers at the U.S. National Institute of Standards and Technology (NIST)[7] in Boulder, Colorado, used beryllium ions in a rather complex experiment that has profound implications.

The experiment used radio waves to stimulate the ions (**Figure 4.3**). The radio waves caused the electrons in the beryllium atoms to jump from the ground state, or level 1, to a higher electron orbit, level 2. By applying the radio impulses for a duration of exactly 256 milliseconds, the investigators found that 100 percent of the ions shifted to this higher energy state (level 2). Similarly, a burst of 128 milliseconds caused only 50 percent of the ions to make the transition, and so on. The researchers developed a sophisticated technique utilizing a laser, which allowed them to measure the exact number of ions in level 1. This laser technique allowed the team to assess the impact of observation, without altering the methodology. As the experimenters radiated the beryllium for the necessary

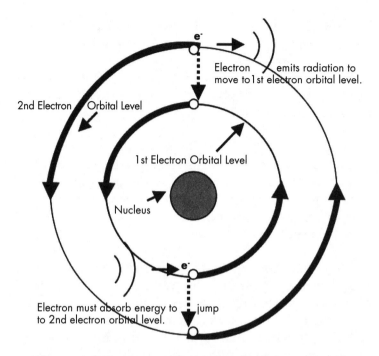

**Figure 4.3 Electrons Emit or Absorb Electromagnetic
Radiation (or photons) as They Jump from
One Atomic Orbital Level to Another.**

256 milliseconds, they determined (with the laser) the
number of electrons in level 1 at varying points in time.
Under classical Newtonian physics, it was expected the
measurements would show 100 percent of the electrons
in level 1 at 0 milliseconds, 50 percent after 128 milliseconds, 25 percent after 192 milliseconds, and 0 percent
after 256 milliseconds. But once again, the act of observation transformed the results.

When the inspectors viewed the ions at 128 milliseconds, half were detected in level 1, as expected. If the
examiners looked four times (e.g., at 64, 128, 192, and 256
milliseconds), fully two-thirds of the ions were still in

level 1 at 256 milliseconds. If the investigators surveyed
the ions every 4 milliseconds for a total of 64 times, almost all the ions remained in level 1. The radio waves
failed to force the electrons into level 2, as expected—
again, as the result of observation. John Gribbin summarized the implications:

> [I]f it were possible to monitor the ions all the
> time then none of them would ever change. If, as
> quantum theory suggests, the world only exists be-
> cause it is being observed, then it is also true that the
> world only changes because it is not being observed
> all the time.[8]

The implications of these experiments are enormous.
Theoretically, neither the laser pulse (in the NIST experiment) nor the photon detectors (in the double-slit experiment) should have interfered in either experiment. It is
apparent, however, that *something* did interact with one
or more components in the tests and alter the outcomes.
Surprisingly, some experts believe that the *act of measuring* is the factor that interfered in these experiments. One
of the most widely accepted theories is that *everything*
exists in a natural waveform *until observed*. At the time of
observation, the *wave collapses into a particle*. At this moment, the state of the entity changes into what we recognize as "reality." As an example, the light we perceive
exists in waveform until it is observed with the eye. Somewhere between the cornea and the brain, the light wave is
converted to a particle. Hence, metaphysical reality ("reality beyond what is perceptible to the senses"[9]) exists as
wave forms; our perception of reality is as particles:

> The idea, which is a natural corollary to the idea
> that an unwatched quantum entity does not exist as
> a "particle", had been around since the late 1970s. A

watched quantum pot, theory says, never boils. And experiments . . . bear this out.[10] (Gribbin)

In the NIST experiment, the act of observation prevented the ions from changing energy levels. The explanation is that electrons can change orbital levels only in their wave forms. Each examination of the ions caused the previously unobserved electron waves to collapse into their particle configurations. As particles, the electrons were unable to jump orbital levels. When, once again, the electrons were not under scrutiny, they returned to their natural wave states and could shift to other energy levels. As such, the more times the experimenters viewed the ions, the fewer the electrons (as waves) that could skip to level 2.[11]

Mathematician John von Neumann, like many, was intrigued by this newfound human power of observation. He systematically inspected every link of the measurement process to identify the probable element that might have altered the outcomes of these experiments. Von Neumann investigated the chain of events leading up to the ultimate collapse of wave to particle. His research arrived at a remarkable conclusion: *All the steps in the series consisted of atoms or electrons in motion except one—the step of human consciousness.*[12]

The world's most renowned and respected scientific minds remain astonished over the implications of these findings. Here are some of their observations:

**Physicist and author Paul Davies:**
According to Bohr, the fuzzy and nebulous world of the atom only sharpens into concrete reality when an observation is made. In the absence of an observation, the atom is a ghost. It only materializes when you look for it.[13]

Does von Neumann's chain end when it reaches the consciousness of a person? This sensational claim has indeed been made by a leading quantum theorist, Eugene Wigner. Wigner suggests that it is the entry of the information about the quantum system into the mind of the observer that collapses the quantum wave and abruptly converts a schizophrenic, hybrid, ghost state into a sharp and definite state of concrete reality.[14]

### Albert Einstein and physicist Ernest Sternglass:

"You see the large tree over there," [Einstein] said. "Now turn your head away. Is it still there?" . . . He was explaining to me one of the principal aspects of the Copenhagen Interpretation of quantum theory that he found particularly unacceptable, according to which an observation or measurement is necessary to bring an object like an electron into definite existence. . .

It was this mysterious, almost magical aspect of the quantum theory that Einstein told me he abhorred, an approach that he deeply felt to be a great mistake, an opinion that I told him I completely shared.[15]

### Astrophysicist and author John Gribbin:

The key concept is the so-called "collapse of the wave function". In seeking to explain how an entity such as a photon or electron could "travel as a wave but arrive as a particle", Bohr and his colleagues said that it was the act of observing the wave that made it "collapse" to become a particle. We can see this at work in the electron version of the experiment with two holes—the electron passes through the experiment as a wave, then "collapses" into a single point on the detector screen.[16]

Quantum interpreters who try to develop these ideas sometimes suggest that the brain itself is . . .

peculiarly suited to collapsing wave functions.[17]

Gribbin further questions what observer is responsible for collapsing the wave functions of *our* minds and physical bodies, and, subsequently, the universe in general.[18] We know that our minds and bodies are capable of operating in the absence of direct observation by others, but our own consciousness could be collapsing those functions. What of the universe? Does the function of the universe collapse as a result of *our* observation or consciousness, or is an outside force involved? These are the questions currently plaguing modern physicists. The presence of an outside observer provides one obvious solution:

> [S]ome cosmologists (among them Stephen Hawking) worry that it implies that there must actually be something "outside the Universe" to look at the Universe as a whole and collapse its overall wave function. Alternatively, John Wheeler has argued that it is only the presence of conscious observers, in the form of ourselves, that has collapsed the wave function and made the Universe exist. On this picture, everything in the Universe only exists because we are looking at it.[19]

> Nothing is real unless we look at it, and it ceases to be real as soon as we stop looking.[20]

> For the Universe to exist as one reality, . . . the Copenhagen Interpretation strictly speaking requires the existence of an observer outside the Universe to do the collapsing of the wave functions.[21]

**Physicist and author Nick Herbert:**
It's a world that's wavelike when unobserved, particlelike upon observation . . .[22]

In most quantum realities the measurement act does not passively reveal some preexisting attributes of quantum entities, but actively transforms "what's really there" into some form compatible with ordinary experience. One of the main quantum facts of life is that we radically change whatever we observe. Legendary King Midas never knew the feel of silk or a human hand after everything he touched turned to gold. Humans are stuck in a similar Midas-like predicament: we can't directly experience the true texture of reality because everything we touch turns to matter.[23]

**Author George Johnson:**
The mathematics used to describe the subatomic realm tells us that, left to its own devices, an electron lacks the very attributes that we, on our macroscopic plateau, consider the very hallmark of existence—a definite position in time and space. It exists, we are told, as a probability wave, a superposition of all the possible trajectories that take on substance only when it is measured, when, as it is often put, an observer collapses the probability wave. How this transformation occurs is one of the deepest mysteries of physics, the so-called measurement problem: How does the rock-solid classical world, in which things occupy definite positions in space and time, crystallize from the quantum haze?[24]

**Physicist and author Gerald Schroeder:**
All the possibilities for existence that fall within the uncertainty of the measurement might actually exist, and only when we make an observation at one specific point do the other possibilities vanish.[25]

**Author Gary Zukav:**

This is the primary significance of the [Heisenberg] uncertainty principle. At the subatomic level, we cannot observe something without changing it. There is no such thing as the independent observer who can stand on the sidelines watching nature run its course without influencing it.[26]

George Johnson feels that it is solely the presence of the detectors that is "simply collapsing the mathematical wave sooner."[27] It is his belief that any measuring device, "a photographic plate as easily as the brain,"[28] may collapse the wave. He noted:

As a final variation on the [double-slit] experiment, imagine that instead of shooting the electrons through a vacuum, we shoot them through a gas of photons dense enough to ensure a reasonable chance that the quantum bullets will interact with the medium. The interference is gone and we get the classical distribution pattern again ... [T]here is no reason to give special status to an observer or to sanctify the measurement act.[29]

However, if one wishes to argue, in this last variation of the double-slit experiment, that the photons acted as a *conscious* medium, then it would still appear that a form of "consciousness" collapsed the wave function. At the same time, I am not naïve enough to think that future evidence might not rebut this premise. However, for now, current evidence suggests, as *one* possibility, that a conscious entity is a prerequisite for waves (the preobserved world) to materialize to the world as we know it.

# 5

# Mind Your Soul

In 1982, Michael Sabom, an Atlanta cardiologist, published research comparing responses of medically knowledgeable individuals without near-death experiences to those of near-death victims without medical backgrounds. The results showed that observations made during NDEs were more accurate, from a medical standpoint, than the responses from the medical control group. Of the twenty-five in the control group, twenty-three made errors in describing a resuscitation. Of the near-death victims, however, none erred in describing their own resuscitations. Melvyn Morse believes this evidence demonstrates "that these people were actually outside their bodies and looking down as they said they were."[1]

Morse also cites the example of an eight-year-old boy

who fell off a bridge while fishing. Jimmy was knocked unconscious in the incident and drowned. The medical records documented neither a pulse nor breathing when police finally pulled Jimmy from the water and initiated CPR. Half an hour later, the helicopter arrived and transported the boy to the hospital. Jimmy was in a coma for two days before he regained consciousness:

> "I know what happened when I fell off that bridge," he told his physician, who related this story to us. He proceeded to describe his entire rescue in vivid detail, including the name of the police officer who tried to resuscitate him, the length of time it took for the helicopter to arrive on the scene, and many of the life-saving procedures used on him in the helicopter and at the hospital.
>
> He knew all this, he said, because he had been observing from outside his body the entire time.[2]

Most researchers of near-death experiences and death-related visions link these phenomena to a very specific region of the brain. Several independent research teams have identified this region as a portion of the *right temporal lobe* known as the Sylvian fissure. When stimulated electrically, this area has induced panoramic life reviews and out-of-body experiences.[3]

Morse described one case in which temporal lobe seizures were used to explain a woman's psychic ability. (This type of seizure may present solely as "hallucinations.") Anne[4] had experienced a life-threatening drug reaction in her youth, which resulted in a cardiac arrest. As doctors worked to resuscitate her, she had an NDE. Following this brush with death, Anne began to have premonitions, which later came to pass. The warnings occurred repeatedly:

When a neighbor's dog was run over she knew it was going to happen because she had dreamed it the night before . . . One time she had a feeling that a person had been hurt in a car accident across town. She told other people about it, and later, the premonition turned out to be true.

Understandably, these visions resulted in significant anguish for her family. Unfortunately, their distress was only to intensify. Anne's nightmare culminated when she divined that her brother was about to be murdered:

Anne saw it in a dream that she told her family about at the breakfast table the morning after she had it. She saw her brother coming to her out of the dark, screaming in pain. He had blood dripping from both hands and an open wound in his belly. He was screaming . . .

On account of the location of the wounds, it was suggested that perhaps she had dreamed of Christ and the crucifixion. Anne insisted she had dreamed of her brother's future.

Two weeks later, her nightmare came true. Burglars broke into her brother's house. He confronted them with a gun and shooting broke out. As he came around the corner of a room holding his weapon in a two-handed grip, one of the burglars fired a shot that passed through both of his hands. A shot also struck him in the abdomen. They left him bleeding on the living room floor and screaming in pain.

Ultimately, Anne sought medical advice and was diagnosed with temporal lobe epilepsy. Treatment of the condition did prove successful, but at a price. The side effects of the medication produced constant drowsiness as the permissible substitute for her psychic prophecies.

Medical evidence supports the temporal lobe as the anatomic site relating to some supernatural phenomena and the NDE. Many, including Morse, feel that this information adds to the evidence that this region of the brain represents the "seat of the soul." As such, they believe that this area is "the spot where the mind, body, and spirit interact."[5]

Paul Davies, on the other hand, believes that identifying a location for the soul is meaningless. Thoughts are intangible actions, and, as such, cannot be confined to locations in space. Excluding the possibility of telepathy, one's thoughts are not accessible to others and must, therefore, exist in a separate dimension or "universe:"[6]

> To say the soul occupies a place means that it exists in some sort of space, either the one we ordinarily perceive, or some other. In that case one may then ask questions about the size, shape, orientation and motion of the soul, all concepts that are totally inappropriate to something composed of thoughts rather than materials.[7]

*Merriam-Webster's Collegiate Dictionary* defines *soul* as "the immaterial essence, animating principle, or actuating cause of an individual life."[8] Consequently, whether one chooses to believe in a physical location in the brain for the soul (or similar entity) or not, most, at least, acknowledge its existence:

> Some societies have believed that the soul represents the highest of human thought, and therefore, it is most abstract and difficult to define. Others have believed that the soul represents the source of life itself, while others have considered the soul only to be the source of afterlife.[9] (Morse)

The debate over the soul's essence is not likely to end soon. More scientists are apt to admit to the presence of the mind (man's ability to reason) than, perhaps, the soul. Nonetheless, whether one believes in the soul or the mind, the process of *thought*, involved in each, remains the unexplained phenomenon. Medically, at least, we know what thought is *not*. It is not a reflexive entity in the brain, like a neurologic reflex arc, but involves reason, judgment, understanding, and, yes, emotion. The miracle of thought continues to leave researchers at a loss for explanations. It is true that the process involves complex networks of neurons, but what is the trigger of the thought process? We know that neurons allow a thought to transmit the signal for arm movement, as an example, but what is the "prime mover" behind thought?

An increasing number of scholars reason that *some* stimulus is required to initiate the thought process (and the soul), similar to the cascade of events involved in today's computers. Just as man represents the "prime mover" behind this artificial intelligence, an analogous stimulus should exist for the soul (or mind). Man programs the computer hardware, writes and installs the software, and operates and controls the various functions. True, a computer may operate, *once programmed*, on its own, but a human still is the *initiating* force behind the computer's actions. What, however, is the source for the soul?

Paul Davies[10] listed several current problems facing research scientists in this field. The brain, consisting of its complex structure of neurons, must act in accordance with the laws of chemistry and physics. Yet, this intricate structure of impulses and molecules feels emotions, recognizes good and evil, initiates thought, and deliberates options—all nonphysical operations. As Davies pointed out, "The existence of [the] mind . . . refutes the reductionist philosophy that we are all nothing but moving mounds of atoms."[11]

> [H]ow does the conscious decision to investigate a noise cause the relevant brain cells to fire? . . . Can the mind somehow reach into the physical world of electrons and atoms, brain cells, and nerves, and create electrical forces? Does mind really act on matter in defiance of the fundamental principles of physics?[12]

Wilder Penfield, from his research in neuroanatomy, concluded that a reservoir of energy apart from the mind must exist if our spirits are to endure beyond death. Our ability to access this energy, albeit unpredictably, during life, may well allow us to unite with it after death. Morse[13] agrees, reflecting that the mind and brain are two separate entities, with the mind representing the brain's conduit to God. The near-death experience is but one result of unlocking this channel and hints at what life after death may be like.

Currently, several theories make the same assertion, claiming that the soul, "the place where the material and spiritual worlds meet,"[14] represents our link to God. If such beliefs are to be taken seriously, one would expect the soul to be capable of interacting outside of space and time, since neither God nor light is restricted to these dimensions. An interaction of this nature would allow instantaneous contact with the past, present, future, and all forms of energy and matter. This concept is compatible with near-death and death-related experiences and is not new:

> "How are the dead raised? With what kind of body do they come?"
> You foolish man! What you sow does not come to life unless it [first] dies.
> And what you sow is not the body which is to be, but a bare kernel . . .

There are celestial bodies, and there are terrestrial
bodies; but the glory of the celestial is one, and the
glory of the terrestrial is another . . .
So it is with the resurrection of the dead. What
is sown is perishable; what is raised is imperishable . . .
It is sown a physical body, it is raised a spiritual
body. If there is a physical body, there is a spiritual
body . . .
For the trumpet will sound, and the dead will be
raised imperishable, and we shall be changed . . .
"Oh death, where is thy victory?" 1 Corinthians
15: 35-55 (RSV)

## The Collective Unconscious

The *collective unconscious,* a theory advanced by psychiatrist Carl Jung, states that wisdom is inherited. If this
is true, then the act of learning is merely recognition of
knowledge that has existed all along. Interpreted on a
broader scale, the collective unconscious is this source of
all knowledge, which exists in a concealed dimension.
This knowledge, for currently unknown reasons, only
sporadically avails itself to us through dreams, visions,
NDEs, and insight:

"I wonder what that building is," my wife said. I
immediately answered with casual and total cer-
tainty, "Oh, that's the Singapore Cricket Club." The
words had popped out of my mouth with utter spon-
taneity. Almost immediately I regretted them. I had
no basis whatever for saying them. I had not only
never been in Singapore before, I had never seen a
cricket club before . . . Yet to my amazement, as we
walked on and came to the other side of the building, which was its front, there by the entrance was a

brass plaque reading Singapore Cricket Club.
How did I know this which I did not know?[15] (Peck)

It is called unconscious because normally we are
unaware of the nonlocal nature of these events. Jung
discovered empirically that, in addition to the Freud-
ian personal unconscious, there is a transpersonal
collective aspect of our unconscious that must operate outside space-time, that must be nonlocal since it
seems to be independent of geographical origin, cul-
ture, or time.[16] (Goswami)

Such is the nature of the collective unconscious. Like
the NDE, if one hasn't had a personal experience involving this phenomenon, accepting its existence can be difficult. Understanding the basic tenets of quantum theory,
however, with or without a religious background, can
bolster acceptance of this realm of collective knowledge.
Recall that quantum theory erases the previous Newtonian
restrictions of space-time and intercommunication. As a
result, qualities such as "superluminal [faster than light]
quantum connectedness"[17] (Bell's theorem) offer explanations for these and other previously unexplained phenomena, including NDEs, visions, and telepathy, as well
as the collective unconscious.

In a related discussion on the Holy Spirit, Scott Peck
explored several of its similarities to the collective unconscious. In his commentary, Peck compared wisdom to a
form of revelation. We typically identify knowledge as
being achieved through life's experiences, education, and
meditation. However, Christian literature characterizes
enlightenment as a type of divine inspiration.[18] Most of
us undoubtedly can recall an instance when we gained
insight in a comparable manner. The truth probably lies
somewhere in between, including both study and revelation.

## Free Will vs. Perfect Determinism

The belief in "perfect determinism" once was one important aspect of the nature of physics. It was held that, given enough information, every future event in the universe could be predicted. Understand, in the world of Newtonian physics, formulas exist to allow the determination of almost any conceivable circumstance. Newtonian physicists believed the only limiting factor for predetermination was the lack of available knowledge:

> Leibniz and Laplace both recognized a puzzling consequence of perfect determinism. If all our laws of motion are in the form of equations which determine the future uniquely and completely from the present, then by a perfect knowledge of the starting state it would be possible for a superbeing to predict the entire future history of the Universe from this raw material.[19] (Barrow)

In a 1990 lecture given at Cambridge, Stephen Hawking analyzed the many aspects of determinism. He concluded that the future *was* predetermined, but that the point was moot—*we* will never be able to determine it.[20]

Other notable scientists believe, with equal conviction, that predetermination is not our fate; i.e., *free will* is genuine. This perspective has developed as the result of quantum theory. Many view the *Heisenberg uncertainty principle* as the main factor mitigating in favor of free will:

> We can never know simultaneously the velocity and position of a subatomic particle. This is the Heisenberg Uncertainty Principle . . . The best we can do is calculate the probability that the electron will appear at a certain place with a certain velocity . . . [21] (Kaku)

In other words, when a physicist identifies the location of an electron, for example, then the velocity cannot also be determined—and vice versa. The problem (or salvation, depending on one's viewpoint) rests with the photon. Researchers utilize light as the method to ascertain an electron's position. As the photon makes contact with the particle, the energy of the light immediately alters the momentum of the electron.[22] No matter what detection method the investigators use, the technique inevitably alters the particle's course. The inability of *any* observer to predict the future outcome of events is the basis for many to advocate free will. With this viewpoint, the question then becomes, "Is God *any* observer?"

Other scientists believe in free will as a result of other features of quantum theory; e.g., the act of observation:

> Since identical conditions do not produce identical results [i.e., the double-slit experiment], the present condition of the universe does not determine the future of the universe. Notwithstanding the ever-present possibility that we may discover the causes underlying phenomena such as these, as we currently understand the world, free will has physics on its side.[23] (Schroeder)

It would appear, barring some unexpected upset of quantum theory, that free will remains intact from the vantage point of the human race. Free will, however, has relevance only to beings locked within a framework of space-time. Such rules do not apply to God.

# 6

# Is Seeing Believing?

We have been taught, throughout our years of education, to believe only that which can be proven. The importance of the scientific method has been emphasized ad infinitum, and we have come to accept that our vision is the ultimate reality. Perhaps the best example of this fallacy lies in the description of the atom. When you thrust your hand into water, the liquid gives way due to the forces of the molecules that constitute each material. The same forces prevent us from placing a fist through a brick wall. What we tend to forget is how little matter actually comprises these forms.

The nucleus of an atom, composed of neutrons and protons, is only about a thousand-billionth of a centimeter in diameter. The electron cloud surrounding the nucleus expands the size to approximately a hundred-millionth of a centimeter.[1] The proton's mass is 1,836 times that of the electron,[2] making the electron's contribution to the mass of the atom quite small (assuming we do not consider the contribution of the electron's velocity or its photons). With these statistics, we can envision the vast amount of space that actually constitutes our world.

In addition, the forces involved in maintaining atomic structure are "inseparable from the structure of [the] particles" (Davies).[3] Electrons repel one another through the exchange of photons. Neutrons and protons attract each other through the exchange of pions, the "glue" of the strong nuclear force, one of the four proposed forces of nature. Physicists continue to investigate these myriad forces, including that which prevents the electrons from spiraling into the nucleus.[4]

Quantum theory supports the principle that all these atomic particles represent just another form of energy. As early as the 1890s, Dutch physicist Hendrik Lorentz first theorized that "mass may only be a manifestation of energy in the region around the source of an electric field."[5] Lorentz was the first to propose that materials (i.e., particles) are really electromagnetic (i.e., waveform) in nature. By his definition, the characteristic of mass is conferred solely by its quality of resisting change in motion, or inertia. This concept agrees with the observation that objects exist *naturally* as waves (electromagnetic radiation), and are transformed into particles only when measured or observed. Hence, we must struggle to remind ourselves that solid objects are purely fields of resistance or force.

Physicist Ernest Sternglass went one step further in his discussion of Lorentz and the electromagnetic nature of all matter. In his own research, dealing with the possibility that all matter is conceivably various reincarnations of electron-positron pairs, Sternglass observed that "all of matter would be a form of light since photons of sufficient energy could turn into electron-positron pairs."[6]

Irrespective of the atom's ultimate structure, should the time come that we are ever able to control these atomic forces, we will easily be able to pass through solid structures such as doors and walls. Note the observation of one near-death victim, as related by Kimberly Clark Sharp:[7]

> She, too, had encountered the Light . . . and remembered sensing music . . .
>
> She explained that she had passed through a wall, knowing that it was composed mostly of space. The most solid objects contained only tiny particles of matter floating in space . . . The limitation of my senses was lifted. I could perceive reality as we know it exists, but cannot normally see it.[8]

Our senses appear less than adequate to reveal the true reality that surrounds us. As we uncover more of the secrets of the universe, we learn more of the limitations of these senses. Much of the universe is invisible to the eye, not due to distance, but because it exists as so-called dark matter. Current evidence indicates that the visible matter, (e.g., stars) may represent only about 1 percent of the total mass of the universe.[9] If we include black holes and nonvisible stars, the percentage rises as high as 10 percent.[10] Consequently, the vast majority of our universe is hidden and entirely unknown to us—possibly beyond anything we can imagine.

Scientists have speculated at what this remaining dark matter could be. Researchers initially thought the mysterious neutrino, a neutral particle, much smaller in mass than the electron, might prove to be the elusive element. Neutrinos react minimally, if at all, with common matter, making them notoriously difficult to measure. However, cosmologists have subsequently dismissed neutrinos as being too small to contribute the necessary mass.

In their continuing search, scientists have hypothesized multiple other particles and entities to explain the missing matter. They include monopoles (north and south magnetic poles that have become separated one from the other), axions (hypothetical subatomic particles with low mass and energy), the "sparticles" predicted by a theory called supersymmetry,[11] weakly interacting massive particles or WIMPs, heavy neutrinos, and even "quark nuggets and little black holes."[12]

Accordingly, there exists much of which we are not aware. Gifted with our five senses, we experience only the three spatial dimensions and time, which many physicists refer to as the fourth dimension. We might compare our limited senses to an allegory told by the Greek philosopher, Plato. Plato spoke of men confined their entire lives to a dark cave. Their eyesight revealed only the shadows cast from a fire onto the cave wall. To them, the shadows represented reality. Socrates, too, felt there was more to be perceived:

> Socrates tells us again we are not to trust our senses, but are instead to look towards our intellects for absolute justice, beauty, and good—all qualities that are dimly visible to the senses.[13] (Wolf)

Our world is obviously more than we sense. One avenue, which is giving us insight into these other realms (to be discussed), is the field of quantum theory. Physicists are attempting to unite the four forces of nature, i.e., the strong nuclear force, weak nuclear force, electromagnetic force,[14] and gravity. These efforts continue to result in new hypotheses to explain these forces and join them into a single theory. Until recently, theorists have succeeded in uniting only three of the four forces; i.e., the strong and weak nuclear forces and the electromagnetic force, but not gravity. Several attempts at the so-far elusive "theory of everything" or "final theory" go by such names as the *standard model*,[15] *Kaluza-Klein theory*,[16] *unified field theory* (Einstein),[17] *grand unified theory (GUT)*,[18] and, more recently, *superstring theory*.[19]

The theory that appears to show the most promise for uniting all four forces is the superstring theory. String theories envision particles, not as points, but as small vibrating strings. What is unusual, at least from the layman's perspective, about superstring and the Kaluza-Klein theories, is their need for added dimensions. The reader may recall that infinities in many equations required the process of renormalization for removal. In these proposed theories-of-everything, the problematic infinities could not be removed except by the addition of extra spatial dimensions—the magic numbers being either nine or twenty-five.[20] Hence, if time is added to the total number of dimensions, the numbers become ten or twenty-six, respectively. If superstring theory is proven, one can envision the number of other realms, of which we have absolutely no comprehension.

Note the observation of theoretical physicist, Michio Kaku, on this subject:

> Claude Lovelace of Rutgers University discovered that the bosonic string (describing integral spins) is self-consistent only in 26 dimensions. Other physicists verified this result and showed that the superstring (describing both integral and half-integral spin) is self-consistent only in ten dimensions. It was soon realized that, in dimensions other than ten or 26 dimensions, the theory completely loses all its beautiful mathematical properties. But no one believed that a theory defined in ten or 26 dimensions had anything to do with reality . . .

Finally, in 1984, Green and Schwarz proved that superstring theory was the only self-consistent theory of quantum gravity and the stampede began.[21]

With the evidence provided up to this point, we must seriously consider the validity of undetectable dimensions. Certainly, it is apparent that there are many forces in action all around us of which we are not cognizant. Kimberly Clark Sharp[22] developed the ability to visualize spirits following her near-death experience. Simultaneously, a doctor also diagnosed her with a medical condition known as narcolepsy. This condition is associated with hypnagogic hallucinations, to which she initially ascribed her visions. Thus, skeptics can attribute her visions to the medical illness. Proponents can credit her gift to the NDE. Sharp's perception into the spiritual dimension continued unabated, however, despite treatment for the condition. So what are we to believe?

Medium and best-selling author James Van Pragh suggests that psychic talents abide, to some extent, within us all and that he "is not unlike anyone else."[23]

> I am often asked if I was born a medium or if I was transformed into one by a terrible illness, or a freak accident that caused some sort of head trauma, or a near-death experience. As hair-raising as those possibilities may be, I cannot claim any one of them as the dramatic moment that introduced me to my life's work . . .
> We all are born with some level of psychic ability. The question is: Do we recognize our psychic abilities and act upon them?[24]

In their books, both Sharp and Van Pragh come across as caring and genuine. I would encourage the reader to keep an open mind—as both cynic and advocate. For those interested, the Committee for the Scientific Investigation of Claims of the Paranormal (CSICOP) maintains an active Web site (www.csicop.org) on the Internet. This site gives an excellent, skeptic's analysis of such claims.

## Ghosts

We and the universe we know may be no more than a bit of static, noise in the cosmic signal . . .[25]
(Johnson)

Although most of us would consider this a rather radical statement, few can deny that many commonly accepted ideas of today were at one time also held to be revolutionary. If we equate our limited sensations to the above "noise in the cosmic" landscape, the analogy becomes apparent. We have discussed NDEs, out-of-body experiences, light, visions of knowledge, and the soul—any of which may serve to glimpse the other dimensions. In many fictional works and short stories, there are descriptions of beings that dwell in one or more of these dimensions. However, this is a nonfiction text. Raymond Moody documented numerous sightings of lost souls or beings as reported by near-death victims whom he interviewed. These testimonials describe these spirits as depressed, confused, bewildered, and confined to a dark purgatorial netherworld, sometimes attempting but unable to make contact with the living:

Several people have reported to me that at some point they glimpsed other beings who seemed to be "trapped" in an apparently most unfortunate state of existence. Those who described seeing these confused beings are in agreement on several points. First, they state that these beings seem to be, in effect, unable to surrender their attachment to the physical world. One man recounted that the spirits he saw apparently "couldn't progress on the other side because their God is still living here." That is, they seemed bound to some particular object, person, or habit. Secondly, all have remarked that these beings appeared "dulled," that their consciousness seemed somehow limited in contrast with that of the others. Thirdly, they say it appeared that these "dulled spirits" were to be there only until they solved whatever problem or difficulty was keeping them in that perplexed state.[26] (Moody)

[T]hey had sad, depressed looks; they seemed to shuffle, as someone would on a chain gang . . . And they seemed to be forever shuffling and moving around, not knowing where they were going, not knowing who to follow, or what to look for . . .
They seemed to be forever moving, rather than just sitting, but in no special direction . . .
They didn't seem to be aware of anything . . .[27] (Moody)

Some persons . . . have noticed certain of these beings apparently trying unsuccessfully to communicate with persons who were still physically alive . . .
You could see them trying to make contact, but no one would realize that they were around; people would just ignore them.[28] (Moody)

Well, it seems more or less that she was trying to get through to them, trying to tell them, seemingly, to do things differently from what they were doing now, to change, to make a change in their life style. Now, this sounds kind of put on, but she was trying to get them to do the right things, to change so as not to be left like she was. "Don't do as I did, so this won't happen to you. Do things for others so that you won't be left like this."[29] (Moody)

One cannot help but think that there may exist a relation between these lost souls reported in NDEs and the authentic reporting of ghosts. Either way, these beings exist in a separate realm. Consider the following observation from physicist, Michio Kaku:

> What kind of beings can walk through walls, see through steel, and perform miracles? What kind of beings are omnipotent and obey a set of laws different from ours?
> Why ghosts, of course![30]

Jung, in his "Psychological Commentary" on The Tibetan Book of the Dead, also discussed ghosts:

> It is a primordial, universal idea that the dead simply continue their earthly existence and do not know that they are disembodied spirits—an archetypal idea which enters into immediate, visible manifestation whenever anyone sees a ghost. It is significant, too, that ghosts all over the world have certain features in common.[31]

My only personal ghost experience occurred in 1985. My wife and I had been living in our new home for about three years. It was located on several acres overlooking the Moshannon Valley of central Pennsylvania. There had been no deaths on the property to our knowledge. One night, around 3 a.m., I awoke from a sound sleep for no apparent reason. At the foot of our bed stood an apparition of white, dressed in a civil war uniform with tassels at the shoulders. I blinked once, and the specter remained. I blinked a second time, and it was gone. As I stared in amazement, my wife screamed out in the night. I roused her from this nightmare, as I have on other numerous occasions. "You're having a nightmare," I said tapping her. "You wouldn't believe what I just saw!" I proclaimed that I had just witnessed my first ghost. "What color was it?" she asked incredulously, adding, "In my dream, I was being chased by a white apparition."

Coincidence? Other explanations? Possibly. So far, this is the only ghost I've witnessed in my life. Nonetheless, it did leave an impression.

## Mental Illness / Senility

When Jung analyzed the liberation of the soul at the time of death ("Psychological Commentary," The Tibetan Book of the Dead), he described how the newly deceased must first come to the realization that they are, indeed, dead. As a part of this recognition, the spirit must sever all bonds with its past consciousness and former reality. Completion of this task is part of the successful transformation into the next world. Jung then compared this detachment from reality to mental illness, an example of a similar disconnection:

> It means the end of all conscious, rational, morally responsible conduct of life . . .
> The psychological equivalent of this dismemberment is psychic dissociation. In its deleterious form it would be schizophrenia (split mind). This most common of all mental illnesses . . . abolishes the normal checks imposed by the conscious mind . . .[32]

Jung went on to warn that psychosis is a real danger to the practice of certain types of yoga, a state in which the mind purposely attempts to separate from its bodily restrictions:

One often hears and reads about the dangers of yoga, particularly of the ill-reputed Kundalini yoga. The deliberately induced psychotic state, which in certain unstable individuals might easily lead to a real psychosis, is a danger that needs to be taken very seriously indeed. These things are really dangerous and ought not to be meddled with in our typically western way.[33]

In summary, "sanity" becomes a label to identify those of us who maintain secure bonds to our body and its physical sensations. Perhaps, some of those labeled "mentally ill" or "senile" by our society are, in truth, closer to metaphysical reality than the rest of us. If their experiences are unencumbered by the physical senses, is it not possible that they could be witnessing other true dimensions?

# 7

# Understanding the Bible

**M**ajor conflicts currently exist between scientific doctrine and stories cited in various religious manuscripts. For our purposes, let us concentrate our examination on the Bible, realizing that similarities exist with several of the world's other major religious texts. In the past, scholars have discredited several biblical ideologies based upon several precepts. Some of the more prominent criticisms have included:

- Creation from nothing
- Creation within six days
- Full creation by God (vs. evolution)
- Longevity of the earliest-mentioned people in the Bible

- Miracles
- Errors and inconsistencies in the text
- The injustices of life permitted by a loving God

This purpose of this chapter is to address these issues.

## The Big Bang

Several theories exist about the creation of the universe. Currently, the prominent scientific explanation is that of the Big Bang. The observation that the universe is now in a state of expansion pleads the case for an increasingly smaller universe in the past. If we continue to look back, we eventually breach the beginning of time itself and reach a point when the entire universe consisted of only a single point in space—the space-time singularity. The Big Bang theory states that nothing existed prior to the instant of this singularity—not time, not the vacuum of space, not space itself. Einstein was able to explain the existence of the singularity; he could not explain its emergence from nothing.[1]

Cosmologists debate whether, and how, a singularity could possibly emerge from a true void, the type of which must have existed prior to the Big Bang. A quantum fluctuation in a vacuum will allow particles to pop in and out of existence (Chapter 3), but even the vacuums of space did not exist before creation. Both science and religion are in agreement on this point.[2] Notwithstanding these irregularities, scientific evidence does support that the universe and all space-time were created from nothing. The puzzle of how is not likely to be resolved anytime soon.

Let us, for a moment, assume the atheistic viewpoint that God was not involved in creation. At the moment of the universe's inception, the forces of nature were forged. Controversy abounds as to whether these "laws" were in place prior to this time. Some insist that these forces are the natural result of the creation of matter and energy at the time of the Big Bang. Others contend that these laws must have been preexistent in order to govern the formation of the singularity:

> It is important to notice that the recent direction of research in cosmology which has sought to provide a mathematical account of the creation of the Universe out of "nothing" implicitly assumes . . . that there pre-exist laws of Nature and other primitive notions like logic prior to the creation of the material Universe . . . It is interesting to consider that if the Universe as a whole is described by a law of Nature like that enshrined in Einstein's general theory of relativity then there must exist a logical structure larger than the physical Universe. Certainly such an assumption is made implicitly in most cosmological studies.[3] (Barrow)

If we accept this statement, then the question arises, what "structure" or entity was the "prime mover" behind the laws of nature? Perhaps matter and energy did arise from something. Perhaps an energy form did exist prior to the Big Bang. Of course, the most popular conception of this entity is God. It has always intrigued me that some scientists will argue vehemently as to why God does not exist, but are equally fervent in their belief that the universe formed from nothing. It is most plausible (even from a scientific standpoint) that all of space-time arose, not from nothing, but from an energy form preexistent to creation and time. This entity consists of infinite energy and, I believe, hints of its existence through the various phenomena discussed in the previous chapters. To seriously consider God as a candidate for this agent, let us examine the other points of contention.

## The Six Days of Genesis

Creation within six days represents the second issue to be addressed. Gerald Schroeder gave an excellent review of a theory that unites the beliefs of both theists and atheists alike; i.e., explaining the six days of creation in cosmic terms. Since the accepted definition of "day" rests upon the rotation of the Earth, the absence of the Earth for the first days presents somewhat of a problem:

> [T]here is no possible way for those first six days to have had an Earth-based perspective simply because for the first two of those six days there was no Earth. As Genesis 1:2 states "And the earth was unformed . . ."
>
> The only perspective available for the entire Six Day period is that of the total universe, one that encompasses the entire creation.[4]

Schroeder went on to explain how, by utilizing the cosmic background radiation (CBR) as his "cosmic clock," the universe was actually created in six "days." The CBR is a pervasive form of residual radiation, left over from the Big Bang, that extends throughout the known universe and corresponds to a temperature of 2.73°K (approximately - 270°C). This 2.73°K represents the current temperature of space, an appreciable reduction from its value .00001 second after the singularity (or 10.9 x 1012 °K). The frequency of the CBR is proportional to its temperature, and since the definition of frequency is based upon time, a universal or cosmic clock can be derived.[5]

Cosmologists have calculated the age of the universe to be approximately 15.75 billion years. This figure is in agreement with the observed age of the oldest stars, i.e., about 16 billion years. Having derived a cosmic reference (the CBR), Schroeder then matched the 15.75 billion-year interval to the six-day time frame of the creation story. The subsequent matches, on a day-by-day basis, correlate fully to the descriptions depicted in Genesis. The comparisons are remarkable **(Table 7.1)**.[6]

Schroeder's handling of the six days of Genesis is nothing short of extraordinary. It is refreshing to see how science can work to support religious doctrine, rather than disparage it.

## The Flaw of Evolution

If we accept the above enhancement to the creation story, we still have the theory of evolution with which to deal. Darwin's theory on the process of evolution (1859) induced one of the most radical upheavals in religious thought of both the nineteenth and twentieth centuries. The reason behind its persuasive power lay in its rationality and simplicity. Mutations are constantly occurring in species, and those mutations that offer advantages to the species will triumph. The key word, here, is species.

Species is defined as "a group of organisms capable of breeding with one another and unable to breed with members of other species."[7] One of the most common explanations for development of a new species is geographic isolation. A unique gene pool may form in a sequestered group as a result of adaptive mechanisms. The members of this new community, if unable to breed with members of the original population, signify development of a new species.[8]

The observation, which continues to add fuel to the evolutionary debate, is that, in all of the fossil record, paleontologists have yet to find an intermediate fossil between two classes or phyla.[9] Further archaeological discoveries may, nonetheless, resolve this issue. As a review, the taxonomic classification comprises species, genus, family, order, class, phylum, and, the highest designa-

| Duration from Bible's perspective: | Duration from Earth's perspective[10]: | Approximate years before Adam at the start of each day: | Bible's Description: | Scientific Description: |
|---|---|---|---|---|
| Day one | 8 billion years | 15¾ billion years | Creation of the universe; light separates from dark (Gen. 1: 1-5) | Big Bang; light literally breaks free as electrons bond to atomic nuclei; galaxies start to form. |
| Day two | 4 billion years | 7¾ billion years | Heavenly firmament forms (Gen. 1:6-8) | Disc of Milky Way forms. Sun forms. |
| Day three | 2 billion years | 3¾ billion years | Oceans, dry land, first life, plants appear (Gen. 1:9-13) | Earth cools; liquid water, first life (bacteria and algae) appear. |
| Day four | 1 billion years | 1¾ billion years | Sun, moon, stars become visible (Gen. 1:14-19) | Atmosphere becomes transparent; photosynthesis produces oxygen. |
| Day five | ½ billion years | ¾ billion years | First animal life; followed by reptiles and winged animals (Gen. 1:20-23) | First multicellular animals; winged insects appear. |
| Day six | ¼ billion years | ¼ billion years | Land animals; mammals, humans (Gen. 1:24-31) | 90-percent massive extinction. Repopulation; including humans. |

**Table 7.1 The Six Days of Genesis[11]**

tion, kingdom (includes the animal and plant kingdoms). Examples of animal phyla include the sponges, flatworms, roundworms, arthropods (e.g., spiders, crustaceans), and the chordates (includes all the animals with backbones). Examples of classes, in the subphylum Vertebrata, include the jawless fishes (e.g., lampreys), the cartilaginous fishes (e.g., sharks), the bony fishes, amphibians, reptiles, birds, and mammals.

Throughout this discussion, keep in mind that the phylogenetic classification is of human design, and, as such, is fraught with some issues. Not everyone is satisfied with the above classification method. The methodology attempts to recreate the evolutionary process by separating organisms into artificial divisions. Controversies arise over the characteristics applied to each category, and the differences required for exclusion. Not surprisingly, the result is that there are various types of taxonomic classifications in existence today.[12]

Despite these contentions, the definition of species has held up well. Darwin, however, contended that new species evolved as a result of natural selection, and that all current life forms originated from past organisms as a result of this process.[13] The major dilemma facing evolutionists today is not the theory, but, rather, the speed of evolution. The fossil record (with its millions of specimens) does not support the rapid pace of evolution. Time, it appears, is the major factor lacking in support of evolution.

During the early formation of the Earth, water and land evolved approximately 3.8 billion years ago. The fossil record reveals that life (bacteria and algae) originated relatively soon after water's appearance. Simple life forms then flourished for the next three billion years. Then, 530 million years ago, life burst forth into the varied phyla we witness today as petrified remains. The development of life to this point was not at all the smooth progression predicted by the theory of evolution.[14] Let us start at the beginning and review the predominant research of the last fifty years that leads up to this conclusion.

There was a famous experiment[15] in 1952, by Stanley Miller at the University of Chicago, who produced amino acids in a flask containing ammonia, methane, hydrogen, and water vapor, all exposed to electric stimulation. These conditions reflected the primordial environment of Earth, with the electrical discharge simulating lightning.

The initial trial resulted in the formation of only a tarlike substance. Subsequent tests generated the amino acids glycine and alanine, but only after altering some of the original variables. This remarkable experiment represented only a beginning. For the development of life, the research was just in its inception. Experiments had yet to produce the remaining eighteen common amino acids, and were far from production of the 170 total amino acids known to exist in life.[16] Also, the amino acids still had to unite into functional chains, or proteins, and were even farther from forming a specific type of protein, the enzyme, required for catalyzing particular biochemical reactions. George Johnson summarized the apparent impossibility of generating life in this manner from a test tube:

At some point we have to stop begging the question and propose some kind of construction mechanism for stringing together amino acids, and the only one we know of requires nucleic acid templates [the complex molecules from which amino acids are created]. But they are due to arrive on the scene only after we have enzymes to make them. And how, without nucleic acid templates, would a protein reproduce? Once a chain of amino acids is strung together and folds up spontaneously into a convoluted glob [of protein], how could it be copied? One would have to posit a mechanism to unravel and read it, amino acid by amino acid. There is no evidence that anything like that has ever existed.[17]

It is helpful to understand the complexity of how proteins are made in the cell. This process[18] entails a complicated operation whereby messenger ribonucleic acid (mRNA) is formed from nuclear deoxyribonucleic acid (DNA). The new mRNA must then diffuse out of the nucleus and travel to a ribosome (made of protein and another RNA, ribosomal RNA). Other forms of RNA, called transfer RNA, then bind particular amino acids consecutively into a specific sequence as defined by the mRNA. Each different sequence of amino acids forms a different, specific protein. In the lowly bacterium alone, scientists have identified about 2,500 different proteins (of which two-thirds are enzymes) and 3,000 different kinds of RNA.[19]

Of special interest, in 2000, IBM announced the development of a special computer, designed specifically to resolve some of the most complex processes of the human body. IBM estimates it will take four to five years to complete assembly of the processor, and that it will perform one quadrillion (one million billion) computations per second. Despite its speed, it is estimated it will take one year just to analyze the mechanism by which a protein folds onto itself.[20]

With all the obvious complexity displayed by even the simplest cell, it should come as no surprise that, more than twenty-five years after Miller's experiment, a retraction appeared in a special 1979 publication of *Scientific American*, titled "Life: Origin and Evolution." This retraction was based on an article written by Harvard professor and Nobel laureate George Wald, who had earlier promulgated Miller's research in defense of evolution.

The retraction unequivocally stated that Wald was wrong, and included a computation performed by author Harold Morowitz. The calculation (from the latter's book, *Energy Flow and Biology*) established that the chance evolution of a bacterium alone was impossible within the lifetime of our universe.[21]

Subsequently, in February 1991, *Scientific American* published a review article by John Horgan on the same subject. In the article, British astronomer Sir Fred Hoyle is quoted, comparing the proposed spontaneous evolution of a unicellular organism to be as probable as the construction of a 747 by a tornado. Horgan recorded that this is a not an uncommon attitude among researchers.[22]

Let us now move forward in time. Unicellular organisms have miraculously emerged from the waters, and multicellular organisms are evolving. Under natural selection, mutations occur randomly. Nature selects which mutations survive (only the "fittest") and which don't. Under these conditions, subsequent, deleterious mutations may eliminate beneficial ones, and vice versa. Consequently, this process takes time. The Precambrian era of initial life began nearly three billion years ago.[23] Simple unicellular life forms flourished. Then, when the Cambrian era commenced approximately 530 million years ago, a plethora of life burst into existence. As Schroeder observed, this explosion of complex, multicellular organisms was not at all the smooth progression predicted by Darwin's theory.[24] The facts indicate the following:

1. The fossil record demonstrates that the vast diversity of life that appeared during the Cambrian era originated within the space of only five million years. To achieve this kind of result, scientists estimate that at least a thousand gene mutations would have been necessary. A change of this magnitude would require hundreds of millions of years.[25]

[One of many known examples supporting this argument is the situation involving the North American and European sycamore trees. These two populations of trees have been isolated from each other for more than 30 million years and still have not evolved into separate species.[26]]

2. The fossil record further indicates an absence of evolutionary transitions for these organisms over this period. "Each of the animals in this era makes its appearance fully developed."[27]

It is difficult, after having grown up under the delusion of Darwin's rationale, to now reformulate one's thinking. Although Darwinian evolution still remains intact to explain minor species-to-species variations (microevolution[28]), creationists are now having to modify their previous views to conform to the appearance of the multitude of new organisms (macroevolution[29]) found as fossils. Two theories which are now being considered are 1) full creation, and 2) directed macroevolution. The term *full creation* denotes the unexplained appearance on Earth of animals already fully developed. Directed macroevolution, in contrast, signifies a special mutational process that is exceedingly enhanced, purposely, to create specific, new animal forms. In this latter process, the mutation rate is remarkably accelerated, compared to that seen today, and most of the beneficial mutations survive.

As Schroeder explained the data, it becomes apparent that even an augmented evolutionary process borders on the impossible within the allotted time. With mutation rates similar to what they are currently, it would take hundreds of billions of generations to generate the human form. Under one accelerated model, let's consider a mutation rate that is increased a millionfold and that no mutations are fatal. Even under these extraordinary circumstances, the evolution of a human being would still require well over a hundred million generations.[30] The fossil record reveals that the human emerged over a period of only seven million years,[31] an inadequate period for even this accelerated model.

Unexpectedly, full creation gains credibility just through the process of elimination. The rational reader will need to remain cautious, maintain an open mind, and assess additional evidence as it becomes available in the future.[32] Modifications to any theory of directed macroevolution might yet salvage this model, but, certainly, the standard theory of evolution appears improbable to explain the development of the new Cambrian life forms.

## Longevity

One longstanding debate involving the Bible entails the characteristic of longevity. Life spans in the Old Testament were sometimes hundreds of years, a stark contrast to the life spans of today. For example, at the time Noah was alive, it was not uncommon for people to live more than 900 years (average 840 years), and sexual maturity occurred between sixty-five to 187 years (average 115 years). These averages are about tenfold higher than those observed today among developed nations.[33] Schroeder observed that, with natural selection in the post-Flood era, enough variation existed in both the ages of sexual maturity and death to permit development of the more recent age attributes. (Note, we are discussing variation within a single species [microevolution], and not macroevolution.) Of interest, both medieval philosopher Moses Maimonides, in the twelfth century, and kabbalist Nahmanides, in the thirteenth century, postulated that alterations resulting from post-Flood conditions and segregation could have "favored . . . shorter life span[s]."[34]

Since this change in longevity is a classic example of

Darwinian microevolution, there is no reason to doubt the possibility of its occurrence. This post-Flood transformation took place over the course of thousands of years. Today, however, we witness many examples of selective Darwinian microevolution, on a remarkably abbreviated time scale, in the farming and cattle industries. One instance is the selective mating of farm animals to achieve preferred, "improved" qualities of stock; e.g., greater size, increased milk production, resistance to disease, etc. This technique is called "artificial selection,"[35] to differentiate it from "natural selection." Researchers have successfully utilized this methodology for plants and animals for years. Additional examples include the accelerated growth of chickens and cattle to market sizes within one month, rather than six, and one year, instead of two, respectively.[36] In today's world, most of what we consume is either the direct or indirect result of such efforts.

## Miracles

A miracle is . . . defined as a phenomenon not explainable by natural law. But that does not mean they are unlawful. Perhaps miracles simply obey laws that we humans generally and currently do not understand.[37] (Peck)

One can not discuss the Bible without commenting on the phenomenon of miracles. Biblical scholars generally come to one or more of the following conclusions regarding their authenticity: 1) The stories are true but have been magnified and exaggerated over the course of time; 2) the stories are at least partially true but are incomplete; or 3) the stories are assumed false but have been promoted to stress a point or moral, similar to a parable.

Many stories, such as those depicted in the Book of Daniel, contain numerous historical errors, thus clouding the text's credibility. Walter Harrelson[38] noted that Belshazzar was not the son of Nebuchadnezzer (Daniel 5:11) and never the king of Babylon (5:1). However, the actual ruler, Nabonidus, had many characteristics that were attributed to Nebuchadnezzer (e.g., madness, visions), and Belshazzar was the son of Nabonidus. Although Belshazzar was never officially king, he acted in this capacity during his father's absence from the throne. Subsequently, Darius the Median (5:30) never replaced Nabonidus or Belshazzar as monarch, but Darius the Great did succeed Cambyses in 521 B.C. Harrelson offered several possible explanations for these errors:[39]

1. The mistakes were naïve or otherwise inadvertent.

2. The author's sole objective lay in conveying the significance or purpose of the story, without regard to the historical facts.

3. The author intentionally misrepresented the facts to give the appearance that he was writing of distant past events.

In other narratives, such as the parting of the Red Sea (or Sea of Reeds, as is more likely), embellishment is probable (Exodus 14:21-31). In this celebrated narrative, God led the Israelites straight to their apparent doom. There they found themselves trapped between the sea and the advancing Egyptians. Scholars are divided on whether the ensuing winds "dried the seabed"[40] or "[drove] back the waters of the sea."[41] Nonetheless, with the aid of darkness and divine guidance, the Israelites proceeded safely across the sea. In the morning, the pursuing Egyptians perished as the winds ebbed and the waters returned. "In the course of time, the story is magnified, the mighty deliverance of Yahweh assuming more miraculous dimensions"[42] (Harrelson).

Additional miraculous phenomena of the Bible are explained or interpreted in other ways. Let us examine just a few examples:

- **The Flood (Genesis 6-8)**
  H. L. Ellison reviewed several theories relating to the great Flood. The description from the Bible is similar to that of a tidal wave inundating the region. As a result, many have proposed that some event released waters restrained in the past by the Armenian Mountains. In 1929, Sir Leonard Wooley advocated that archaeological discoveries at Ur proved existence for the Flood. S. H. Langdon subsequently claimed a similar find at Kish. Other discoveries followed at Uruk and Shuruppak. However, research soon revealed that the relevant rock strata from each location was from a different era.[43] Hence, it appears that multiple floods have involved this area, but which one, if any, represents the great Flood remains in dispute.

- **Destruction of Sodom and Gomorrah (Genesis 19: 1-38)**
  D. F. Payne depicted the entire Jordan Valley as a primary fault line in the Earth's crust. An earthquake in this region would not be wholly unexpected and could explain the resulting destruction of these two towns. Although a rationalization for the resulting transformation of Lot's wife is more complex, "[f]alling debris could have encased [her]."[44]

- **The burning bush (Exodus 3: 1-12)**
  Various explanations have included St. Elmo's fire, plant gas, and optical illusions. Robert Gordon, without discounting such accounts, believes the significance lies in the fire's symbolism.[45]

• **The plagues of Egypt leading up to the Passover (Exodus 7-13)**

Conjecture for the plagues vary on the spectrum of illustrative allegories to actual events. Most historians agree that the plagues could have indeed occurred. Flooding of the Nile, especially between July and September, will not uncommonly stir up plentiful amounts of red clay (i.e., the "blood" of plague #1), producing the "Red Nile."[46] Heavy rains in the Nile Valley may spawn the appearance of countless frogs (plague #2). Swarms of locusts (#8) may invade from Arabia, destroying all known vegetation. Sandstorms, known to last up to three days, could explain the darkness of the ninth plague. The remaining afflictions (lice, flies, murrain, boils, hail) are also possible, realizing that some are more probable than others. The Passover, however, is the focal point of all the preceding accounts, and remains largely unexplained except as a parable of thanksgiving and remembrance.[47]

• **Flight from Egypt/provision of quail and manna (Exodus 16: 13-31)**

In the spring, quail may fly over the Sinai during migrations from Africa and Arabia. Gordon observed that these are birds, which typically "fly quite close to the ground and, especially when exhausted, are easy prey."[48]

Possible candidates for the manna include a product from the juice of the tamarisk bush[49] and "the Arabic mann which is found in parts of the Sinai peninsula in early summer[,] . . . an edible excretion produced by certain insects."[50]

• **Flight from Egypt / water from a rock (Exodus 17: 1-7)**

During the flight through the Sinai, God instructed Moses to strike a rock to end the Israelites' exhaustive search for water. In this region of the world, it is not unusual for springs to emanate from rocks. One such spring, Ayin Musa ("the spring of Moses"), exists today in Edom.[51]

- **The Messiah**
  To Christians, of all the miraculous events related in the Old Testament, the prophecies of the coming Messiah are some of the most enthralling:

> For to us a child is born, to us a son is given;
> and the government will be upon his shoulder,
> and his name will be called
> "Wonderful, Counselor, Mighty God, Everlasting
> Father, Prince of Peace."
> Of the increase of his government and of peace
> there will be no end,
> upon the throne of David, and over his kingdom,
> to establish it, and to uphold it
> with justice and with righteousness from this time
> forth and for evermore. Isaiah 9: 6-7 (RSV)

> But you, O Bethlehem Ephrathah, who are little to
> be among the clans of Judah,
> from you shall come forth for me one who is to be
> ruler in Israel,
> whose origin is from of old, from ancient days.
> Micah 5: 2

Mention of these miracles and prophecies, as well as errors in the Bible, is made to bring attention to both the strengths and weaknesses of this great book. Not only do its passages reflect tremendous wisdom and beauty, but apparent flaws in the text remind us as well that it is but a historical document, written by human hands. At the same time, we must keep in perspective our own limitations at viewing history. Our own resources and references are incomplete, and we lack all the necessary knowledge for appropriate understanding. [As an aside, take, for example, the stories surrounding the alleged improprieties of Thomas Jefferson (in office 1801-9) with his slave, Sally Hemings. Journalist James Callender printed the first known allegation of the affair in 1802. Throughout the next two centuries, historians generally discredited such accusations. However, in 1998, DNA testing revealed that Jefferson or his brother could have been the father of at least one of Heming's children. It is clear that new developments in science are forever altering our view of history.]

We are constantly confronted with multiple explanations and criticisms of the Bible. The repetition and consistency of Christ's many miracles, from one book to another, is particularly noteworthy. Historians chronicle, however, that a single source was probably largely responsible for the first three books (or "Synoptic Gospels," Matthew, Mark, and Luke) of the New Testament. In contrast, the Fourth Gospel of John is distinct, and scholars believe an independent author is responsible. Despite the discrepancy in authors, the descriptions of Christ's miracles is similarly recounted in both accounts; e.g., changing water into wine, healing the sick, feeding the five thousand, walking on water, raising Lazarus from the dead, and, of course, the Resurrection.

Skeptics of miracles will always remain, and this distrust is understandable. Future historians will undoubtedly look at our modern-day research and unexplained testimonials with equal skepticism. Take, for example, some of the miraculous cases of "supernatural rescue," as documented by Raymond Moody. In these accounts, unexplained forces intervene to rescue individuals who find themselves in fatal circumstances. The victims falter on the brink of certain death when, unexpectedly, a light or voice provides a means of escape. As previously noted, these NDEs restore or intensify the spirituality, or, in other ways, radically impact the lives of those involved:[52]

1. In the book, *A Man Called Peter,* Catherine Marshall detailed how the subject averted death by heeding a voice, which prevented his walking off a cliff in foggy weather. The experience catalyzed his transformation to become a minister.[53]

2. Another man related to Dr. Moody his experience, of becoming trapped in an enormous chemical chamber at his work site. As he cried out for help, a mixture of pressurized acid and steam entered the enclosure:

> The heat of all this was terrific. I yelled, "Let me out of here. I'm getting trapped." I had gotten as far as I could into a corner, and put my face into the corner, but the stuff was so hot that it was burning me through my clothing. So, at that time I realized that in just a matter of minutes I would be scalded to death.
>
> I guess it was in my weakness or whatever that I gave up. To myself, I just said, "This is it, I'm a goner." I could not see, and the heat was so intense that I could not open my eyes. I had my eyes closed the whole time. But it seemed that the whole area lit up with a glow. And a verse of Scripture that I had heard all my life, that had never meant too much to me, "Lo, I am with thee always," came from a direction which later turned out to be the only way out.
>
> I couldn't stand to open my eyes, but I could still see that light, so I followed it. I know that my eyes were closed the whole time, though. The doctor didn't even treat my eyes later. No acid got in them . . .[54]

3. In one more case, a woman was resuscitated as the result of a near-fatal infection:

The doctors had all given up on me. They said I
was dying . . . I got to the point where I was feeling
the life going out of my body . . . I could still hear
what everyone was saying, though I couldn't see
anything. I wished I could live to raise my children
and to play a part in their lives . . .
    That's when I heard God's voice talking to me. He
had the most loving gentle voice . . . I know I wasn't
out of my head, as some people might think . . . I
could hear the voices of the others in the room, in
the background . . . but I could sense his voice, too,
and it was so overwhelming. He told me that if I
wanted to live, I was going to have to breathe . . .
and so I did, and when I took that one breath, I
started to come back. Then he told me to breathe
again, and I was able to take another breath, and the
life came back into my body . . .
    The doctors were amazed. They had all given me
up, and naturally they hadn't heard the voice I had.
They couldn't understand what happened.[55]

Moody cautioned that not all NDEs display the positive elements found in the above scenarios (e.g., the recognition of imminent death, the interaction with God or
the Light, the sense of love, the receipt of life-saving
instructions, and the resultant, favorable change in one's
perspective on life), but noted, "they have occurred in a
sizable number of my cases."[56]

## Suffering

[I]t may be that God finished His work of creating
eons ago, and left the rest to us. Residual chaos,
chance and mischance, things happening for no reason, will continue to be with us . . . In that case, we
will simply have to learn to live with it, sustained

and comforted by the knowledge that the earthquake and the accident, like the murder and the
robbery, are not the will of God, but represent that
aspect of reality which stands independent of his
will, and which angers and saddens God even as it
angers and saddens us. (Kushner)[57]

Harold Kushner, author of *Why Bad Things Happen to
Good People*, gave an excellent analysis of suffering in
today's world and concluded that God allows free will in
our world. This deduction is in stark contrast to the religious fundamentalist, who ascribes too literal a transla-
tion to many passages of the Old Testament—that is, our
suffering is the direct result of our sins:

"Think now, who that was innocent ever perished? Or where were the upright cut off?
As I have seen, those who plow iniquity and sow
trouble reap the same." Job 4: 7-8 (RSV)

The righteous is delivered from trouble, and the
wicked gets into it instead. Proverbs 11: 8

The wicked are overthrown and are no more, but
the house of the righteous shall stand. Proverbs 12: 7

No ill befalls the righteous, but the wicked are
filled with trouble. Proverbs 12: 21

Tell the righteous that it shall be well with them,
for they shall eat the fruit of their deeds.
Woe to the wicked! It shall be ill with him, for
what his hands have done shall be done to him.
Isaiah 3: 10-11

A more liberal interpreter might translate the action of

these passages to the soul or afterlife without implying an earthly cause-and-effect relationship.

In his own search for justice and purpose in life, the author of Ecclesiastes concluded that God is in unquestionable control over our lives. Donald Fleming, in his research of this Old Testament text, summarized the document by noting that our struggles in life are futile; i.e., the future is predetermined. The author sought for meaning in life by pursuing the contrasting pursuits of wisdom and then pleasure, to no avail. God's intention is that we enjoy life and engage in work that is gratifying and satisfying. We should accept happiness as a gift, but should not pursue pleasure as our sole objective in life. Humankind will never understand, nor be privy to, God's ultimate plan. As such, our role is to accept, as best we can, whatever fate befalls us.[58]

Others assume a point of view midway between Kushner and the author of Ecclesiastes, believing that God intervenes selectively. It is with such a perspective that we should begin review of the Book of Job:

> There was a man in the land of Uz, whose name was Job; and that man was blameless and upright, one who feared God, and turned away from evil . . .
> And the Lord said to Satan, "Have you considered my servant Job, that there is none like him on the earth, a blameless and upright man, who fears God and turns away from evil?"
> Then Satan answered the Lord, "Does Job fear God for nought? Hast thou not put a hedge about him and his house and all that he has, on every side? Thou hast blessed the work of his hands, and his possessions have increased in the land. But put forth thy hand now, and touch all that he has, and he will curse thee to thy face." And the Lord said to Satan, "Behold, all that he has is in your power;

only upon himself do not put forth your hand."
So Satan went forth from the presence of the Lord.
Job 1: 1,8-12 (RSV)

In the Book of Job, God gave Satan permission to test
Job. This story is the quintessential representation of suffering by the righteous. In the above example, God allowed Satan to bring about Job's suffering. It is of interest
to note that, despite different attitudes on why suffering
occurs, both Kushner and the author of Job agree on how
people should respond to their suffering. Notwithstanding apparent inequities in life, Kushner believes we
should continue to love God by understanding that He
does not intervene in events on Earth. Job, on the other
hand, promotes an "acceptance of the will of God that is
able to bless God both for what he has given and what he
has taken away (1:21), both for good and for harm
(2:10)[59]" (David Clines).

Despite this "acceptance of the will of God," Job did
not restrain himself from speaking out against Him. Job
complained to God of the unjust actions, and, in doing so,
advanced that God is the sole executor of his destiny. For
this recognition, God honored Job over his three friends:

"[M]y servant Job shall pray for you [the friends],
for I will accept his prayer not to deal with you
according to your folly; for you have not spoken of
me what is right, as my servant Job has." Job 42: 8
(RSV)

And the Lord restored the fortunes of Job . . . and
the Lord gave Job twice as much as he had before.
Job 42: 10

Comparing the above outcome with Kushner's viewpoint shows how two authors are able to reach the same

conclusion (to continue to love God despite injustice) using two diametrically opposed arguments. Kushner voiced God's noninterference in human events, while Job's author acknowledged His direct interaction in human affairs. Either way, the moral is the same: We should recognize God as creator and accept our circumstances. It is the response to adversity that distinguishes one's faith. The book of Job also surprisingly indicates that a human display of anguish and emotion is permissible before a loving God:

> "Therefore I will not restrain my mouth; I will speak in the anguish of my spirit; I will complain in the bitterness of my soul.
> Am I the sea, or a sea monster, that thou settest a guard over me?
> When I say, 'My bed shall comfort me, my couch will ease my complaint,'
> then thou dost scare me with dreams and terrify me with visions,
> so that I would choose strangling and death rather than my bones. . .
> If I sin, what do I do to thee, thou watcher of men? Why hast thou made me thy mark? Why have I become a burden to thee?
> And why dost thou not pardon my transgression and take away my iniquity?" Job 7:11-15, 20-21 (RSV)

Satan played an unequivocal role in Job's torment. At this phase of religious history, Lucifer ("the light bearer") still functioned as an angel of God. His duties included testing the faith of humanity and keeping God apprised of conditions on Earth.[60] The Book of Revelation documents Satan's subsequent rebellion:

> Now war arose in heaven, Michael and his angels

fighting against the dragon; and the dragon and his angels fought, but they were defeated and there was no longer any place for them in heaven.

And the great dragon was thrown down, that ancient serpent, who is called the Devil and Satan, the deceiver of the whole world—he was thrown down to the earth, and his angels were thrown down with him. Revelation 12: 7-9 (RSV)

At the end of time, the devil rises up in one last desperate attempt to overthrow God, but is again defeated:

And I saw the beast and the kings of the earth with their armies gathered to make war against him who sits upon the horse and against his army.

And the beast was captured, and with it the false prophet who in its presence had worked the signs by which he deceived those who had received the mark of the beast and those who worshipped its image. These two were thrown alive into the lake of fire that burns with brimstone. Revelation 19: 19-20 (RSV)

The question of the devil's existence is a common topic of debate by scholars. Scott Peck, M.D., believes the devil is a true entity, based on his personal dealings with exorcisms. In his book, *People of the Lie,* Peck allocates an entire chapter to possession and exorcism. During fifteen years of psychiatric practice, he never encountered a case that even resembled possession, emphasizing the rare nature of this phenomenon:

But the fact that I had never seen a case did not mean such cases, past or present, were out of the question. I had discovered a large volume of literature on the subject—none of it "scientific." Much of

it seemed naïve, simplistic, shoddy, or sensational.
A few authors, however, seemed thoughtful and sophisticated, and they invariably stated that genuine
possession was a very rare phenomenon.[61]

Peck had to actively search out and submit inquiries to
multiple contacts before locating even possible candidates of possession. The first two cases suffered from
standard psychiatric afflictions and were not true posses-
sions:

> In both cases, the major distinction in differential
> diagnosis was between possession and multiple per-
> sonality disorder. In these cases there were two
> distinguishing features. In multiple personality
> disorder the "core personality" is virtually always
> unaware of the existence of the secondary personali-
> ties—at least until close to the very end of prolonged,
> successful treatment. In other words, a true disso-
> ciation exists. In these two cases, however, both pa-
> tients were either aware from the beginning or were
> readily made aware not only of the self-destructive
> part of them but also that this part had a distinct and
> alien personality . . .[62]

Peck did, however, witness what he believed was actual demonic possession with two subsequent cases. The
resulting study of these patients and their backgrounds
led to some unexpected findings:

> Something now must be said of the utmost im-
> portance. While both these patients demonstrated
> blatantly evil secondary personalities, they were not
> evil people . . .
> Not only did the core personality of each seem
> healthy, it seemed unusually good and potentially

saintly. In fact, I admired both of these people very much even before the exorcisms. As I have indicated, they came to exorcism precisely because they had struggled against their possession for some years. A mature psychiatrist team member said, following one of the exorcisms, "I have never seen a person of such courage." Indeed, I have reason to suspect that the potential holiness of these two people was one of the reasons for their possession . . .[63]

We witness in these excerpts that, like Job, the victims need not be evil people. This point cannot be overemphasized.

Since the cases of possession are extraordinarily complex, the reader should refer to Peck's *People of the Lie* and, especially, to Malachi Martin's *Hostage to the Devil* for more detailed descriptions.[64] Nevertheless, the following discussions, through Peck's rational vantage point, help to demystify the possibility of this demonic phenomenon:

I don't hope to convince the reader of Satan's reality. Conversion to a belief in God generally requires some kind of actual encounter—a personal experience—with the living God. Conversion to a belief in Satan is no different. I had read Martin's book before witnessing my first exorcism, and while I was intrigued, I was hardly convinced of the devil's reality. It was another matter after I had personally met Satan face-to-face.[65]

As Peck spoke of his personal experience with the exorcisms, he first noted the proficiency of the teams, each consisting of at least seven professionals of both sexes. There were no secondary motives involved. All freely volunteered their time, working twelve to twenty hours per day, as many days as required (in Peck's cases, three and four days, respectively). Unfortunately, most churches are reticent to sanction, lend support to, or actively participate in the "healing" of such cases. As such, the only prerequisite demanded of each team member was the demonstration of love.[66]

Let us now examine the nature of the expulsions through an engaging synopsis by Peck:[67]

> As a hardheaded scientist—which I assume myself to be—I can explain 95 percent of what went on in these two cases by traditional psychiatric dynamics . . . But I am left with a critical 5 percent I cannot explain in such ways. I am left with the supernatural—or better yet, subnatural. I am left with what Martin called the Presence.

Simultaneously, Peck also became acutely aware of another's attendance in the room—God's.

Prayer is a critical factor in the success or failure of the operation. As Peck noted, "These prayers are for God or Christ to come to the rescue, and each time I had a sense that God did just that."

As the process continued, the team permitted itself to communicate only with the patient's prepossession personality or that of the demonic, but not with any vague admixture of the two (the Pretense). The success of the exorcism was thus dependent upon "the final stripping away of the Pretense so as to come face-to-face with the demonic." To achieve this goal, restraint of the patient was often necessary. One case required restraint for two hours, while the other necessitated restriction for more than twenty-four hours.

The emergence of the beast in both of these cases is compared:

[A]n expression appeared on the patient's face that could be described only as Satanic. It was an incredibly contemptuous grin of utter hostile malevolence ... Yet when the demonic finally revealed itself in the exorcism of this other patient, it was with a still more ghastly expression. The patient suddenly resembled a writhing snake of great strength, viciously attempting to bite the team members. More frightening than the writhing body, however, was the face ... Despite these frequent darting moments, what upset me the most was the extraordinary sense of a fifty-million-year-old heaviness I received from this serpentine being. It caused me to despair of the success of the exorcism. Almost all the team members at both exorcisms were convinced they were at these times in the presence of something absolutely alien and inhuman. The end of each exorcism proper was signaled by the departure of this Presence from the patient and the room.

Both expulsions proved successful. However, as in the reality of everyday life, the end of each exorcism did not mark the beginning of a happy-ever-after scenario. The "attacks" were to reoccur with the beast(s) attempting to regain control. The demon renewed its efforts with incessant provocation and intimidation. One difference did emerge. As one patient described, previously the voices controlled him. Now, he was in control of them.

Most of us have experienced times—far short of possession, which may have made us ask whether some malevolent influence was responsible for our own actions. Hence, the phrase, "The Devil made me do it," takes on added meaning. Has the Devil evolved merely as an excuse for our mortal frailties, or is it a true entity, capable of interfering in our daily lives?

In a wonderful quotation befitting the subject of this

text, Peck commented, "I have an inchoate sense that these exorcisms were not just isolated events but somehow almost cosmic happenings."[68]

The one conclusion that one can draw from this analysis into suffering is this: Suffering is not necessarily the product of sin. I say "necessarily" only to distinguish that some suffering and guilt are rightfully the direct result of sin; e.g., guilt felt for stealing, murder, etc.

At this juncture, we are ready to move forward and examine the evolution of individual spiritual growth and development.

## Spirituality

Life is not a problem to be solved but a mystery to be lived.[69] (Peck)

As most people have witnessed in their own lives, it is normal to go through phases of spiritual belief, doubt, unbelief, and, then, acceptance once again. This progression represents just one of the many growth-and-learning processes of life. This questioning and search for answers is a continual part of development and should be encouraged.

Peck, in *The Different Drum*, listed a common pattern or evolution of spiritual maturation. He cautioned, however, that each individual is unique, and variations of development abound:

### Peck's Phases of Spiritual Growth:

| | |
|---|---|
| Stage I: | Chaotic, antisocial |
| Stage II: | Formal, institutional |
| Stage III: | Skeptic, individual |
| Stage IV: | Mystic, communal |

**Table 7.2 Spiritual Development[70]**

Stage I is characterized as the earliest phase of growth. Children and psychopaths (no relationship intended) fall into this category. The goals of such individuals are characteristically self-serving and manipulative. As Peck noted, these people are "generally incapable of loving others . . . [a]lthough they may pretend to be loving (and think of themselves that way)."[71]

Stage II represents the stage that many of us pass through as early disciples of our parents' teachings and principles. At this stage, God is identified as loving, but also punitive—like "a giant benevolent Cop in the Sky."[72]

At some point, the individual begins to question the meaning and (in)justice of life. At this point, one has entered Stage III. Its constituents include the nonbelievers, or, at least, the skeptics. As Peck observed, these people are not typically antagonistic or unsociable, but are often loving, caring individuals (and parents) committed to community interests. In their steadfast pursuit of the truth, they may also become dedicated scientists and researchers.[73]

When enough questions are answered to their satisfaction, the Stage III-ers may come to accept that there is a Supreme Design(er) of our universe. At this crossroad, they have entered the final stage, IV. Peck made use of the term "mystic" for this phase. Note how he defined this word almost in quantum physics' terms:

"Mysticism," a much maligned word, is not an easy one to define. It takes many forms. Yet through the ages, mystics of every shade of religious belief have spoken of unity, of an underlying connectedness between things: between men and women, between us and the other creatures and even inanimate matter as well, a fitting together according to an ordinarily invisible fabric underlying the cosmos.[74]

# 8

# The Grand Design

Thus far, facts in support of a design for the universe (e.g., the attributes of light, nonlocality, human observation, and the evidence of the fossil record) continue to mount. Let's look now at how the laws and constants of nature, which govern our world, were intentionally calibrated for the creation of our specific universe.

In 1992, the Cosmic Background Explorer Satellite (COBE) completed collection of its data on the cosmic heat radiation (see Chapter 7, "Six Days of Genesis") left over from the Big Bang. What COBE revealed was the presence of unexplained inconsistencies or "wrinkles" in the distribution of the background radiation. The existence of these variations provided a rationale for the formation of our galaxies, groups, and superclusters within the estimated 16-billion-year age of the universe. Without this key clumpiness in the initial conditions of the universe, cosmologists estimate the development of the galactic clustering would have taken tens of billions of years, instead of sixteen. Hence, this discovery was good news for astronomers and the scientific method. Scientists find, however, that accounting for the irregularities in the cosmic radiation is not as easy as its discovery. The search for a satisfactory explanation continues. George Smoot, head of the COBE project, initiated a media frenzy when he divulged that the discovery of the radiation pattern was like unveiling God.[1] One apparent conclusion: The evolution of our universe appears to have been purposely accelerated.

In 1974, Brandon Carter published a concept, now referred to as the *strong anthropic principle*.[2] This principle infers that life exists on Earth because the physical laws of our universe are precisely what they are. Viewed another way, the reverse is also true: If the forces of nature were different, we would not be here. The implications are not as apparent as they seem. The cynics argue that our universe is not so exceptional. Had a divergent universe evolved, we simply would not exist. Alternatively, infinite, disparate universes (each characterized by its own distinctive constants of nature) may currently exist in tandem with ours, and, if so, are devoid of life (at least, as we know it). Proponents of this latter philosophy believe we just happen to inhabit that particular universe that exhibits the physical laws that we observe.

There are, however, a number of scientists who remain in awe over the observed schema of *our* universe. These partisans either perceive our universe to be purposely singular and unique, or otherwise judge life (humankind, in particular) to be very special.

The precision to which the existence of life hinges on the observed forces of nature is nothing short of extraordinary, as illustrated by observations by some of today's leading scientists:

> [H]ad the original energy of the Big Bang explosion been less, the universe would have fallen back onto itself long before there had been time to build the elements required for life and to produce from them intelligent, sentient beings. Had the energy been more, it is quite possible that the density would have dropped too swiftly for stars and galaxies to form. These and many other details were so extraordinarily right that it seemed the universe had been expressly designed for humankind.[3] (Owen Gingerich, astronomer)

> If the density of the universe one second after the big bang had been greater by one part in a thousand billion, the universe would have recollapsed after ten years. On the other hand, if the density of the universe at that time had been less by the same amount, the universe would have been essentially empty since it was about ten years old.[4] (Stephen Hawking, physicist)

It is well established that, within the nuclear furnaces of the stars, hydrogen is converted to helium. Heavier elements, like carbon and oxygen, form from the resulting helium. However, formation of the heavy elements beyond iron (e.g., gold, lead, and uranium) requires the *energy* produced in a *supernova* explosion. The subsequent *release* of these elements into space (necessary for formation of the planets and, hence, life) depends upon the *blast* from these supernovae:

> Without the manufacture and dissemination of these elements, there could be no planets like the

Earth. Life-giving carbon and oxygen, the gold in our banks, the lead sheeting on our roofs, the uranium fuel rods of our nuclear reactors—all owe their terrestrial presence to the death throes of stars that vanished well before our sun existed. It is an arresting thought that the very stuff of our bodies is composed of the nuclear ash of long-dead stars.[5] (Paul Davies, mathematical and theoretical physicist)

Scientists have, in addition, discovered that the formation of the life-providing elements (e.g., hydrogen, carbon and oxygen) would not have been possible without the precision provided by the constants of nature. Production of the known elements demands a series of complex atomic reactions. Even small modifications to the fundamental laws would have precluded elemental creation. For example, a minor alteration in the relationship between the strong and weak nuclear forces would have arrested the formation of hydrogen. The lack of hydrogen would prohibit formation of water and the organic compounds. Likewise, a change in the electromagnetic force would transform the distinct chemical properties of carbon and water. Any one of these changes would have negated the prospect for life:[6]

Had the resonance level in the carbon been 4 percent lower, there would be essentially no carbon. Had that level in the oxygen been only half a percent higher, virtually all of the carbon would have been converted to oxygen. Without the carbon abundance, neither you nor I would be here now.

I am told that Fred Hoyle, who together with Willy Fowler found this remarkable nuclear arrangement, has said that nothing has shaken his atheism as much as this discovery.[7] (Gingerich)

Hoyle discerned that the nuclear forces seemed to have been specifically manipulated for elemental production.[8] He is far from alone in this belief.

What impresses many scientists is not so much the fact that alterations in the values of the fundamental constants would change the structure of the physical world, but that the observed structure is remarkably sensitive to such alterations. Only a minute shift in the strengths of the forces brings about a drastic change in the structure . . .

The list of numerical "accidents" that appear to be necessary for the observed world structure is too long to review here.[9] (Davies)

Oxford mathematician Roger Penrose has calculated some intriguing statistics relating to the formation of the universe. From one series of computations, he figured an odds ratio of $(_{10}10)^{30}$ to one against the likelihood that the universe formed by chance.[10] In another instance, he amassed all the odds against the possible generation of life, dating back to the time of the Big Bang's inception. His arithmetic revealed the staggering odds of $(_{10}10)^{123}$ to one. As Gerald Schroeder summarized, "That is one out of a billion billion billion, etc., repeated more than a billion billion times."[11]

Questions raised in Chapter 7 scrutinized whether the forces or constants of nature existed prior to the Big Bang. If none existed, then what factors governed and influenced the creation of this singularity, the seed of our universe? If controlling forces preexisted, then the universe did not appear from "nothing." Many believe that this organizing force is God. Indeed, a host of scholars and scientists, in addition to those already cited, believe the vast weight of evidence favors a planned universe:

[T]he origin of life appears to be almost a miracle, so many are the conditions which would have to be satisfied to get it going.[12] (Francis Crick, Nobel prize winner, biochemist)

If we could play God, and select values for these natural quantities at whim by twiddling a set of knobs, we would find that almost all knob settings would render the universe uninhabitable. Some knobs would have to be fine-tuned to enormous precision if life is to flourish in the universe.[13]

It is in that province [the "fundamental constants" of nature] that we find the most surprising evidence for a grand design.[14] (Paul Davies, physicist)

In some mysterious way, God is the creator of all the living forms in the evolutionary process, and particularly in hominid evolution of human persons, each with the conscious selfhood of an immortal soul.[15] (John C. Eccles, Nobel Prize winner for physiology and medicine)

Nevertheless, just as I believe that the Book of Scripture illumines the pathway to God, so I believe that the Book of Nature, with its astonishing details—the blade of grass, the *Conus cedonulli*, or the resonance levels of the carbon atom—also suggest a God of purpose and a God of design. And I think my belief makes me no less a scientist.[16] (Owen Gingerich, astronomer)

However, many scientists exist in a philosophical solitude that rejects Purpose in favor of "Blind Chance." . . . They ignore experimental evidences of Purpose in all circumstances of life, as well as historical evidence of its impact on many aspects of life in the Christian West, including the nurture of science.[17] (Daniel H. Osmond, physiologist)

If we have eyes to see, the anthropic principle will speak to us of the signs of God's purpose present in the remarkable potentiality with which our universe has been endowed in the basic ground of its physical process.[18] (John Polkingborne, physicist)

In particular, we must come to understand God as acting as creator and redeemer both of and through the processes of nature as well as those of history.[19] (Robert John Russell, physicist, theologian)

Modern physics and cosmology impact in a number of ways upon our understanding of a God who purposefully creates and sustains the world.[20] (Russell Stannard, physicist)

As with the countless stars, we too are a universe of complexity, a deeper reality, to be known fully, not in material but in spiritual terms, as an image of the Creator who purposed it so to be.[21] (John Templeton, investor and author)

Lastly, note Stephen Hawking's viewpoint on this subject:

It is now generally accepted that the universe evolves according to well-defined laws. These laws may have been ordained by God, but it seems that He does not intervene in the universe to break the laws. Until recently, however, it was thought that these laws did not apply to the beginning of the universe. It would be up to God to wind up the clockwork and set the universe going in any way He wanted. Thus, the present state of the universe would be the result of God's choice of the initial conditions.[22]

As previously noted, some cosmologists advocate the concurrent existence of an infinite number of parallel universes. Unique laws of nature would distinguish each of these other, far different worlds. These proponents maintain that our universe just happens to exhibit the necessary constants by chance. In other words, out of an infinite number of possible universes, at least one is likely to have formed with the constants (and life) that we observe.

The evidence presented in this text argues that the universe is as we know it because it was designed that way.

# 9

# End of Existence

$\mathbf{A}$s we peer out into the night sky, seldom do we appreciate that our view is of the remote past. The visible universe is literally a look into distant history. As we gaze at the Andromeda galaxy, it is difficult to accept that we are viewing its appearance from two million years ago (i.e., two million light-years away). In contrast, the center of our own galaxy, the Milky Way, is only a mere 20,000 light-years removed. Little of what we see from the night sky is as it presently exists, so vast is the universe.

When we direct our sight to the Sun (through a protective filter, of course), its light is already eight minutes old. If the Sun were to suddenly explode, we wouldn't know it until eight minutes later.

The Earth orbits at a distance of 150 million kilometers

from the Sun. Of all the planets circling the Sun, only Earth journeys in an unlikely orbit. As planets form from their stellar debris, a recognized pattern of planetary distribution usually occurs. The planetary nuclei collect about the central star in an exponential pattern. Typically, each planet forms at a distance approximately twice as far from the Sun as its preceding neighbor. This is true in our solar system for all but one noticeable exception—Earth. Neptune, although close, and Pluto do not quite obey the expected arrangement due to the eccentricity of the latter's orbit.[1] Pluto's orbit, in fact, is so elliptical, that it regularly crosses the path of Neptune. Astronomers have even conjectured that Pluto might be an escaped moon of Neptune or a massive comet.[2]

The measured distances of the planets from the Sun (in millions of kilometers) are as follows: Mercury, 58; Venus, 108; *Earth, 150*; Mars, 228; asteroids (minor planets), mean 405 (range 315 - 495); Jupiter, 778; Saturn, 1427; Uranus, 2871; Neptune, 4497 [Pluto, 5914].[3]

This oddity of Earth's position constitutes another of Earth's many mysteries. Consider that Earth's peculiar orbit and axial tilt allow for the seasons and temperate climate that we experience. Earth is the *only* known planet to feature a temperature range permitting the existence of liquid $H_2O$, rather than just its gaseous or solid states. Without these "accidents," our atmosphere, oceans, and, of course, life would never have formed. Had water and life appeared on Mars, instead, scientists would merely observe that this chance event followed as the result of the planet's calculated, expected distance from the Sun. Still, this is not the case. Rather, Earth appears in an unforeseen orbit, at just the exact, mandatory distance from the Sun to allow the development of all the extraordinary conditions necessary for life. Is this not a prime example of directed evolution?

Let us examine the force that was the controlling factor

in Earth's development, i.e., gravity. Gravity is the force that initially drew each planet into configuration and now maintains each in its orbit about the Sun. It is the one force that physicists still struggle to fit into a "theory of everything" (Chapter 6). What physicists know of gravity is quite limited. It *is* known that gravity relates *directly* to an object's mass and *inversely* to the square of its distance from another object. Physicists still conjecture about the mechanism by which this force is transmitted. They have theorized that the force is conveyed via the *graviton*,[4] and evidence in support of its existence is mounting.

Not long after developing his general theory of relativity, Einstein foresaw the discovery of gravitational waves, which travel at the speed of light. Like light, these waves travel without the requirement of an ether, or medium. Unlike light (a form of electromagnetic radiation), gravity is the weakest of the four known forces. Even the presence of Earth barely affects passage of the feeble gravitational wave. (In contrast, a metal screen almost completely absorbs the common radio wave.) In theory, it is the motion of one mass in relation to another that incites the generation of gravitons. Physicists calculate the gravitational energy, generated by Earth orbiting the Sun, for instance, to be on the order of only one milliwatt.[5]

Of special interest is the belief by physicists that gravity is a *negative* energy force, which exactly balances the positive energy of all matter in the universe. By counterbalancing matter, gravity allows the total overall energy of the universe to equal zero and, hence, permits the universe's creation from "nothing."

If, at the end of time, the universe collapses in on itself in the Big Crunch, gravity will be the instrumental factor. Not only is gravity one of the primary influences allowing for our creation, but it *may* also be the cause of our ultimate demise. I say "may" because there are two main theories of the end of our universe: 1) the Big Crunch, and 2) continued expansion. Astronomers have verified, since the first discovery by Edwin Hubble in the 1920s, that the universe is expanding. The question of whether the universe will start to contract rests on whether there is enough mass in the universe to stop the current expansion. The current visible matter (e.g., stars) makes up only *one percent* of the necessary mass to halt the present expansion. It is theorized that unseen dark matter (e.g., dim stars and black holes) may make up an additional 9 percent. Hence, we still have only 10 percent of the total mass required to initiate a contracting universe. Despite this shortcoming, many cosmologists feel that there are forms of undiscovered "dark" matter waiting to be discovered, which may account for the missing 90 percent. As noted in Chapter 6, neutrinos, monopoles, axions, and "sparticles" represent possible candidates.

Many scientists believe an additional factor, known as *inflation,* played an important role in the formation of the early universe. This process, if proved, requires that enough mass exists in the universe to effect the Big Crunch.[6] Steven Hawking determined, "the inflation that seems to have occurred in the early universe . . . [involved] an increase in size by a factor of at least a million million million million million times in a tiny fraction of a second."[7]

Then again, there are alternate theories that have argued *against* the Big Crunch, not the least of which is the apparent lack of matter. One such theory involves the characteristic known as *entropy.* Entropy is known in the physics world as the *second law of thermodynamics* and states that, as time goes on, the cosmos experiences increased disorder of organization. Examples include the effects of weather (e.g., soil erosion), disease, aging, general wear-and-tear, and other destructive processes (including black holes).

Original theories on entropy concluded that, since our current, expanding universe conforms to the second law, a contracting universe might exhibit reverse tendencies. Specifically, some physicists considered that a contracting universe would actually be a universe of increasing *order*, an obvious breach of entropy. Stephen Hawking, at one time, also fell into this camp:

> At first, I believed that disorder would decrease when the universe recollapsed. This was because I thought that the universe had to return to a smooth and ordered state when it became small again. This would mean that the contracting phase would be like the time reverse of the expanding phase. People in the contracting phase would live their lives backward: they would die before they were born and get younger as the universe contracted . . .[8]

Additional research and discoveries soon caused Hawking to recant. The Big Crunch would *not* violate entropy. Paul Davies agreed with Hawking's reassessment, assuming, that is, that a black hole represents a smaller version of the Big Crunch:

> The black hole represents the equilibrium end state of a gravitating system, corresponding to maximum entropy.
> Although the entropy of a general gravitating system is not known, work by Jacob Bekenstein and Stephen Hawking, in which the quantum theory is applied to black holes, has yielded a formula for the entropy of these objects. As expected, it is enormously greater than the entropy of, for instance, a star of the same mass.[9]

Hence, we find ourselves back at square one. The

universe's end is no clearer now than before. Will it be total annihilation in the Big Crunch or an ever-expanding universe? Is there a paradox that both an expanding, as well as a contracting universe, are considered to represent increasing entropy?

The controversy over entropy is far from settled. Some scholars have argued that the existence of life violates the second law of thermodynamics. The organizing factor involved in the creation of life seems, at least outwardly, to be a prime contradiction to the second law. Unfortunately, physicists must dismiss this argument. Despite humankind's progress and ability to achieve some semblance of order, research indicates that increasing disorder is the unavoidable result. Just the act of reading this book has expended thousands of calories. In the process, your body has transformed food (ordered energy) into heat, carbon dioxide, and water (disordered energy).

Roger Penrose, mathematical physicist, voiced his amazement, not at the effects of entropy but, rather, its origin: "What *should* surprise us is that entropy gets more and more ridiculously tiny the farther and farther that we examine it in the past!"[10] In other words, what caused the initial organization from which disorder has evolved? Add this to the growing list of arguments for a grand design.

However, despite entropy's ceaseless advance, science remains unable to classify consciousness into this scheme of orderliness. Gary Zukav related one interesting viewpoint on why the second law may not apply to the thought process. Entropy is defined as increasing disorder *over time*. Zukav observed that the second law does not apply to quantum processes, such as those recognized for subatomic particles, because time loses its relevance at this level (recall that light is a quantum process and is not restricted by time). Entropy does prevail over molecules, however. The question begging an answer, then, is whether consciousness is a molecular or quantum process. If it is a quantum process, and we have seen evidence to that effect (e.g., superluminal communication), then this law would not apply to the process of thought:

> If we can experience the most fundamental functions of our psyche, and if they are quantum in nature, then it is possible that the ordinary conceptions of space and time might not apply to them at all (as they don't seem to apply in dreams).[11]

So there is the *possibility* that entropy may not apply to *all* aspects of the complex, organizing process known as life. Nonetheless, disorder will prevail in its ultimate hold over the universe, and, as such, will perpetrate its inevitable finale. Even if destiny calls for perpetual expansion, physical life will not survive the resulting environment:

> For the stars that do escape, and for any gas or dust that avoids a black hole death, the reprieve is only temporary. If the grand unified theory is correct, the nuclear material of this cosmic flotsam is unstable, and will evaporate away after about $10^{32}$ years. The neutrons and protons decay into positrons and electrons, which then start to annihilate with each other [liberating light] and any further electrons. All solid matter thus disintegrates.[12] (Davies)

If, on the other hand, the Big Crunch is our final fate, then total annihilation is the consequence. Even in this scenario, two options are conceivable: 1) the universe disappears from existence forever (or at least until another "quantum fluctuation" occurs), or 2) at some unimaginable density, it bounces back into being as another Big Bang, repeating ad infinitum. This latter depiction has received the designation, the "oscillating"[13] or "cyclic universe."[14]

However our universe ends is purely speculation as we await further discoveries.

What is apparent is the uniqueness of our universe, which appears to have been specifically designed for the evolution of life on this special planet. We have established the occurrence of too many accidents to be explainable by serendipity alone.

# 10

# Conclusions

He is not God of the dead, but of the living . . .

Mark 12:27

The preceding chapters have provided evidence that our current existence is the result of a higher authority, not serendipity. This Supreme Entity is not removed from our lives, but, rather, avails His wisdom and knowledge at unpredictable and unexplained times.

I have attempted to give the viewpoints of renowned experts in their respective fields, in addition to my own, to stress the available facts. I am an ardent advocate of the biblical admonition, "[S]eek, and you will find" (Matthew 7: 1). I do believe God supplies answers for those committed to finding the truth. I would stress that one needs to maintain an ever-open mind, however, for future changes in data and information. Knowledge is ever dynamic. Even well-respected theories rotate through cycles of intense skepticism, as well as great support. I fully expect that some of the findings in this text may lose favor over the next many years. If this is the result only of cyclical biases, then the facts will establish these theories over time. On the other hand, scientific findings may prove one or more views to be flawed. If this proves to be the case, then I welcome the additional information as an avenue toward the ultimate truth. Religious and scientific tenets have been modified throughout time immemorial, and I believe the future will lead to an even closer union of these two disciplines. I would caution against altering one's convictions based only upon speculative information, especially when common sense dictates otherwise. As times call for adaptations to current beliefs, do so with good judgment and the appropriate research.

The abundance of data presented here in support of an omnipotent and omniscient Force is compelling. Remember what *is* known. We exist as intelligent, thinking beings who also are capable of occasionally experiencing the other, hidden dimensions known to exist through quantum theory. These dimensions include the realm of spirits (good *and* evil) and the domain of knowledge—all free from the restrictions of space-time.

Our reality is the world of atoms, a world consisting mostly of space, but proven to harbor *infinite* energy. Our environment seethes with a myriad of forces and energies—not the true substance that we envision.

Hypothetically, animals (including humankind) could have evolved similarly to plants, i.e., exhibiting *only* the necessary, reflexive activities for their immediate needs (e.g., hunger). In such a world, wisdom and thought would not exist (unless one considers the Venus flytrap or ape to be wise). Knowledge is a gift, to be pursued and treasured. Providence has destined a special purpose for this race known as humanity.

Let us reconsider the pertinent discussions from this

text that denote the existence of a higher authority:

1. Evidence for a grand design (e.g., the finely tuned constants of nature, Earth's peculiar position in our solar system, directed evolution, and the organization from which entropy has evolved) points to a design in Creation.

2. *Current* information (the fossil record) indicates Darwin's theory of evolution to be flawed, leaving full creation and directed macroevolution as the remaining alternatives.

3. Creation from "nothing" and the six days of Genesis appear to be literal and factual, in astrophysics terms.

4. The soul represents humankind's direct link to God and the spiritual world, and is the possible element that induces the collapse of the wave function (producing our day-to-day reality).

5. Our limited senses prevent us from experiencing the other, concealed, spiritual dimensions predicted by quantum theory. On occasion, God unveils these dimensions as the collective unconscious, visions, and death-related experiences.

6. Superluminal communication is proven and is exhibited in near-death experiences, death-related visions, visions of knowledge, the collective unconscious, and the laboratory (the double-slit and EPR experiments). Actions on Earth are now recognized to have immediate, albeit unknown, ramifications elsewhere in the universe. Our Creator has linked the entire cosmos.

7. The near-death experience exemplifies our closest preview of what may await us beyond death. Space-time restrictions disappear. Warmth, peace, love, knowledge, and understanding supplant suffering and ignorance.

8. Science chronicles light as one of the first features of the known universe, and, predictably, the last.

Einstein positioned light as the cornerstone of the special theory of relativity and all modern physics.

Both electromagnetic radiation (including light) and God exist outside of time and have infinite energy (or power). Light exhibits an uncanny and unexplained awareness (or consciousness) of its surroundings and reacts accordingly. This communication occurs instantaneously.

There are countless references to light (as God or Christ) in the world's many religious texts, including the Bhagavad Gita, *Koran*, Book of Mormon, *Apocrypha*, *Kabbalah*, and the Old and New Testaments of the Bible. It is unlikely that all these references occurred purely coincidentally.

Light is one of the major features of the near-death experience and represents the presence of God and/or, for Christians, Christ.

Light has revealed its incredible association not only with God, but also all matter (living and nonliving), consciousness, and knowledge. At the speed of light (and simultaneous cessation of time), the "Eternal Now" becomes reality. The present becomes synonymous with the past and future. In this circumstance, enlightenment commences where space-time culminates. In the physical world, everything is ultimately reducible to the infinite essence of light—the alpha and the omega—that medium that imparts earthly vision and warmth also conveys absolute love, knowledge, and understanding.

## One Hypothesis

Some may conclude, from the evidence presented here, that God exists, at least in part, in the form of light. If this is true, then God is far from hidden from our lives, and, instead, permeates every aspect of our existence. (Even in total darkness, approximately 400 million photons are present in every cubic meter of space throughout our universe.[1]) I would further suggest that God's essence pervades *all* things. This theory emanates from the fact that all matter will eventually degrade (given enough time) into light, or, as Hendrik Lorentz suggested, matter is really just another form of electromagnetic radiation. The finding that matter exists naturally in wave form, prior to any kind of measurement (and "collapse of the wave function"), likewise supports this conclusion. Accordingly, terms to describe the Almighty, such as "infinite, timeless, omnipresent, and omniscient" are literal and factual.

It is also interesting to speculate upon the poorly understood phenomena of black holes, where the dimensions of space-time are distorted beyond comprehension, and light is not allowed escape. Equally valid arguments could be made in defense of a black hole being a divine province versus, on the other extreme, the corollary of Hell.

I am not naïve enough to think that humankind is capable of uncovering the innermost secrets of the Great Almighty. Rather, the hypotheses stated here are merely that—speculation upon the workings of a very special but mysterious universe.

Science continues to make daily strides into our understanding of the world, life, and our very being. The special attributes of light represent just one facet of this diamond of life. I believe the Lord has unveiled these properties to us for a reason: *Consciousness* is not limited only to life forms. God is with us as a constant presence in our lives, permeating all matter, substance, and thought. The evidence exists for us to recognize this Power. It is up to us to verify and affirm this relationship in our everyday lives, and to lead our lives, as best we can, in accordance with the Creator's wishes.

Author Kimberly Clark Sharp, following her near-death experience, succinctly related what she discovered from her journey:

The Light gave me knowledge, though I heard no words . . . "Why are we here?" To learn. "What's the purpose of life?" To love.[2]

Oddly, science, the once-great nemesis of religion, is now its friend.

### Claim to Believe

We claim to believe in Him
And eternity of the soul.
Why, then, should we all fear Death
If God is in control?

We weep, we grieve, we gnash our teeth
When a loved one's end is near.
Shouldn't we, instead, be envious?
Instead, it's Death we fear.

We suffer life; God knows it's true.
We pray to avert Death's due.
Isn't it really rather selfish
Of me and you?

Does it really make any sense
To congregate and confess
Before God of our truest sin . . .
Of doubt in Him, I guess?

If in our faith we truly trust,
And in God we believe,
Wouldn't it surely make more sense
To sing and dance, instead of grieve?

# Endnotes

*Introduction*

ᶦPeck, M.D., M. Scott. *The Different Drum*. New York: Simon and Schuster, 1987, p. 188.

ᶦᶦMoody, Jr., M.D., Raymond A. *Life After Life*. New York: Bantam Books, 1975.

ᶦᶦᶦCalder, Nigel. *Einstein's Universe*. New York: Greenwich House, 1979.

ᶦᵛZukav, Gary. *The Dancing Wu Li Masters*. New York: Bantam Books, 1979.

ᵛMoody, Jr., M.D., Raymond A., op. cit., and *Reflections on Life After Life*. New York: Bantam Books, 1977.

*Chapter 1: Adventures in Death*

[1]Moody, Jr., M.D., Raymond A., *Life After Life*, New York, Bantam Books, 1975.

[2]Moody, op. cit., p. 21-23.

[3]Moody, Jr., M.D., Raymond A. *Reflections on Life After Life*. New York: Bantam Books, 1977, p. 107.

[4]Sharp, Kimberly Clark. *After the Light*. New York: William Morrow and Company, 1995, p. 26.

[5]Sharp, op. cit., pp. 168-69.

[6]Moody, Jr., M.D., *Reflections on Life After Life*, p. 110.

[7]Morse, M.D., Melvin, with Paul Perry. *Closer to the Light*. New York: Ivy Books, 1990.

[8]Ibid., pp. 139-41.

[9]Morse, M.D., Melvin, with Paul Perry. *Transformed by the Light*. New York: Villard Books, 1992, pp. 95-7.

[10]Evans-Wentz, W.Y. (ed.). *The Tibetan Book of the Dead*. New York: Oxford University Press, 1960, p. lvi.

[11]Ibid., p. 36.

[12]Ibid., pp. lxxiv-lxxix.

[13]Kaplan, J.D. (editor). *Dialogues of Plato*. New York: Washington Square Press, 1950.

[14]Ibid., pp. 377-386.

[15]Morse, *Transformed by the Light*, p. 101.

[16]Ibid., pp. 103-4.

[17]Sharp, op. cit.

[18]Ibid., op. cit., p. 97.
[19]Morse, *Closer to the Light*, p. 58.
[20]Ibid., p. 60.
[21]Ibid., p. 66.
[22]Moody, *Life After Life*, p. 144.
[23]Moody, *Reflections on Life After Life*, p. 44-45.
[24]Ibid., p. 45.
[25]Ibid., p. 46.
[26]Moody, *Life After Life*, p. 143.

*Chapter 2: Light*

[1]Moody, Jr., M.D., Raymond A. *Life After Life*. New York: Bantam Books, 1975, pp. 58-60.
[2]Morse, M.D., Melvin, with Paul Perry. *Closer to the Light*. New York: Ivy Books, 1990, pp. 131-133.
[3]Morse, M.D., Melvin, with Paul Perry. *Transformed by the Light*. New York: Villard Books, 1992, p. 196.
[4]Morse, *Closer to the Light*, p. 134.
[5]Negatively charged elementary particles.
[6]Quanta of light.
[7]Kaku, Michio. *Hyperspace*. New York: Oxford University Press, 1994, p. 104.
[8]Energy = mass times the square of the speed of light.
[9]Gribbin, John. *Schrodinger's Kittens and the Search for Reality*. New York: Back Bay Books, 1995, pp. 35-36.
[10]Ibid., pp. 68-72.
[11]Zukav, Gary. *The Dancing Wu Li Masters*. New York: Bantam Books, 1979, pp. 130-32.
[12]Adapted from Zukav, op. cit., p. 131.
[13]Gribbin, *Schrodinger's Kittens*, op. cit., p. 79.
[14]Gribbin, John. *In Search of Schrodinger's Cat*. New York: Bantam Books, 1984, p. 191.
[15]It is possible that particles given the name of tachyons conceivably exist. These hypothetical particles cannot go *slower* than the speed of light.
[16]Weinberg, Steven. *Dreams of a Final Theory*. New York: Vintage Books, 1993, pp. 108-109.
[17]Gribbin, *In Search of Schrodinger's Cat*, pp. 256-257.
[18]Weinberg, Steven, op. cit., pp. 113-4.

[19]Davies, Paul. *God & the New Physics*. New York: Touchstone Books, 1983, p. 155.

[20]Hawking, Stephen. *A Brief History of Time*. New York: Bantam Books, 1988, p. 157.

[21]Goswami, Ph.D., Amit, with Richard E. Reed and Maggie Goswami. *The Self-Aware Universe*. New York: Jeremy P. Tarcher/Putnam, 1993, p. 49.

[22]Johnson, George. *Fire in the Mind*. New York: Vintage Books, 1995, p. 75.

[23]Schroeder, Gerald L. *The Science of God*. New York: Free Press, 1997, p. 164.

[24]Adapted from Gribbin, *In Search of Schrodinger's Cat*, pp. 16, 167.

[25]Schroeder, Gerald L, op. cit., p. 155.

[26]Zukav, p. 63.

[27]Gribbin, John. *In Search of Schrodinger's Cat*, p. 164.

[28]Gribbin, John. *Schrodinger's Kittens*, p. 114.

[29]Goswami, op. cit., p. 75.

[30]Davies, Paul. *About Time*. New York: Touchstone Books, 1995, p. 169.

[31]Adapted from Davies, *About Time*, p. 169.

[32]Adapted from Davies, *About Time*, p. 169.

[33]Adapted from Davies, *About Time*, p. 171.

[34]Adapted from Davies, *About Time*, p. 171.

[35]Ibid., p. 169-71.

[36]Goswami, op. cit., p. 73.

[37]Davies, *God & the New Physics*, p. 204 .

[38]*Home Religious Library*. Nashville: The Southwestern Company, 1977.

[39]Goodspeed, Edgar J. (trans.). *The Apocrypha*. New York: Vintage Books, 1959, p. 191.

[40]Ibid., p. 342.

[41]Matt, Daniel C. *The Essential Kabbalah*. Edison, New Jersey: Castle Books, 1995, p. 90.

[42]Ibid., p. 110.

[43]*The Book of Mormon*. Salt Lake City: The Church of Jesus Christ of Latter-Day Saints, 1981, pp. 178-9.

[44]Ibid., p. 522.

[45]Dawood, N.J. (translator). *The Koran*. New York: Penguin Books, 1997, p. 249.

[46]Ibid., p. 391.
[47]Edgerton, Franklin (trans.). *The Bhagavad Gita*. New York: Harper Torchbooks, 1944, p. 56.
[48]Ibid., p. 56.
[49]Peck, M.D., M. Scott. *People of the Lie*. New York: Touchstone Books (Simon and Schuster), 1983, p. 203.
[50]Ibid., p. 209.
[51]Moody, *Reflections on Life After Life*, pp. 15-16.

*Chapter 3: Faster than a Speeding Bullet*

[1]Cramer, John. "The Transactional Interpretation of Quantum Mechanics," *Reviews of Modern Physics*. 1986; 58(3): 647-687.
[2]Ibid., p. 661.
[3]Herbert, Nick. *Quantum Reality*. New York: Anchor Books, 1985, p. 199.
[4]Ibid, pp. 211-12.
[5]Ibid., pp. 226-27.
[6]Ibid., pp. 212-27.
[7]Ibid., pp. 136-41.
[8]Adapted from Herbert, op. cit., p. 218.
[9]Ibid., p. 138.
[10]Adapted from Herbert, op. cit., p. 218.
[11]Adapted from Herbert, op. cit., p. 218.
[12]Ibid., p. 64.
[13]Ibid., p. 223.
[14]Ibid., p. 230.
[15]Moody, Jr., M.D., Raymond A. *Reflections on Life After Life*. New York: Bantam Books, 1983, p. 9-10.
[16]Ibid., p. 10-11.
[17]Ibid., p. 14.
[18]Sharp, Kimberly Clark. *After the Light*. New York: William Morrow and Company, 1995, p. 239.
[19]Zukav, Gary. *The Dancing Wu Li Masters*. New York: Bantam Books, 1980, p. 298.
[20]Hawking, Stephen. *A Brief History of Time*. New York: Bantam Books, 1990, p. 157.
[21]Gribbin, John. *Schrodinger's Kittens and the Search for Reality*. New York: Back Bay Books, 1995, p. 123
[22]Herbert, op. cit., p. 69.

# SEEKING INFORMATION ON

**holistic health, spirituality, dreams,
intuition or ancient civilizations?**
**Call 1-800-723-1112, visit our Web site,
or mail in this postage-paid card for a FREE
catalog of books and membership information.**

Name: _____

Address: _____

City: _____

State/Province: _____

Postal/Zip Code: _____ Country: _____

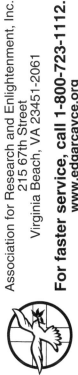

Association for Research and Enlightenment, Inc.
215 67th Street
Virginia Beach, VA 23451-2061

**For faster service, call 1-800-723-1112.**
**www.edgarcayce.org**

PBIN

# BUSINESS REPLY MAIL

FIRST CLASS   PERMIT NO. 2456   VIRGINIA BEACH, VA

POSTAGE WILL BE PAID BY ADDRESSEE

**ASSOCIATION FOR RESEARCH
AND ENLIGHTENMENT INC
215 67TH STREET
VIRGINIA BEACH VA   23451-9819**

[23]Davies, Paul. *The Last Three Minutes*. USA: Basic Books, 1994, p. 19.

[24]A state of infinite density representing an infinite gravitational field and infinite space-time curvature (Davies, Paul. *About Time*. New York: A Touchstone Book, 1995, p. 131).

*Chapter 4: Beyond Observation*

[1]Gribbin, John. *Schrodinger's Kittens and the Search for Reality*. New York: Back Bay Books, 1995, p. 116.

[2]Adapted from Gribbin, John. *In Search of Schrodinger's Cat*, New York: Bantam Books, 1984, pp. 16, 167.

[3]Adapted from Gribbin, John. op. cit., pp. 16, 167.

[4]Schroeder, Gerald L. *The Science of God*. New York: Free Press, 1997, pp. 156-7.

[5]Gribbin, *Schrodinger's Kittens*, p. 13.

[6]Herbert, Nick. *Quantum Reality*. New York: Anchor Books, 1985, p. 226.

[7]Gribbin, *Schrodinger's Kittens*, pp. 133-35.

[8]Ibid., pp. 134-35.

[9]*Merriam-Webster's Collegiate Dictionary*. Springfield, MA: Merriam-Webster, Inc., 1993, p. 731.

[10]Gribbin, *Schrodinger's Kittens* p. 132.

[11]Ibid., p. 135.

[12]Herbert, op. cit., p. 148.

[13]Davies, Paul. *God & the New Physics*. New York: Touchstone Books, 1983, p. 103.

[14]Davies, *God & the New Physics*, p. 115.

[15]Sternglass, Ernest J. *Before the Big Bang*. New York: Four Walls Eight Windows, 1997, pp. 53-54.

[16]Gribbin, *Schrodinger's Kittens*, p. 10.

[17]Ibid., p. 151.

[18]Ibid., p. 15.

[19]Ibid., pp. 15-16.

[20]Gribbin, *In Search of Schrodinger's Cat*, p. 173.

[21]Gribbin, *Schrodinger's Kittens*, p. 163.

[22]Herbert, op. cit., p. 69.

[23]Ibid., p. 194.

[24]Johnson, George. *Fire in the Mind*. New York: Vintage Books, 1995, p. 112.

[25]Schroeder, op. cit., p. 148.

[26]Zukav, Gary. *The Dancing Wu Li Masters*. New York: Bantam Books, 1979, p. 112.

[27]Johnson, op. cit., p. 143.

[28]Ibid., p. 148.

[29]Ibid., p. 164.

### Chapter 5: Mind Your Soul

[1]Morse, M.D., Melvin, with Paul Perry. *Closer to the Light*. New York: Ivy Books, 1990, pp. 119-20.

[2]Ibid., pp. 120-21.

[3]Ibid., pp. 118-19.

[4]Morse, M.D., Melvin, with Paul Perry. *Transformed by the Light*, New York: Villard Books, 1992. pp. 93-5.

[5]Ibid., p. 195.

[6]Davies, Paul. *God & the New Physics*, New York: Touchstone Books, 1948, p. 73.

[7]Davies, *God & the New Physics*, p. 80.

[8]*Merriam-Webster's Collegiate Dictionary*. Springfield, MA: Merriam-Webster, Inc., 1993, p. 1123.

[9]Morse, *Closer to the Light*, p. 109.

[10]Davies, *God & the New Physics*, pp. 75, 78, 229.

[11]Ibid., p. 229.

[12]Ibid., p. 75.

[13]Morse, *Closer to the Light*, p. 127.

[14]Ibid., p. 126.

[15]Peck, M.D., M. Scott. *The Road Less Traveled*. New York: Touchstone Books (Simon and Schuster), 1978, p. 252.

[16]Goswami, Ph.D., Amit, with Richard E. Reed and Maggie Goswami. *The Self-Aware Universe*. New York: Jeremy P. Tarcher/Putnam, 1995, p. 128.

[17]Zukav, Gary. *The Dancing Wu Li Masters*. New York: Bantam Books, 1980, p. 298.

[18]Peck, M.D., M. Scott. *The Different Drum*. New York: Simon and Schuster, 1987, p. 76.

[19]Barrow, John D. *Theories of Everything*. New York: Fawcett Columbine, 1991, p 53.

[20]Hawking, Stephen. *Black Holes and Baby Universes and Other Essays*. New York: Bantam Books, 1993, p. 139.

[21]Kaku, Michio. *Hyperspace.* New York: Oxford University Press, 1994, p. 114.

[22]Sternglass, Ernest J. *Before the Big Bang.* New York: Four Walls Eight Windows, 1997, p. 31.

[23]Schroeder, Gerald L. *The Science of God.* New York: Free Press, 1997, p. 157.

*Chapter 6: Is Seeing Believing?*

[1]Davies, Paul. *God & the New Physics.* New York: Touchstone Books, 1983, p. 146.

[2]Barrow, John D. *Theories of Everything.* New York: Fawcett Columbine, 1991, p. 126.

[3]Davies, *God & the New Physics*, p. 147.

[4]Sternglass, Ernest J. *Before the Big Bang.* New York: Four Walls Eight Windows, 1997, p. 53.

[5]Ibid., p. 21.

[6]Ibid., p. 137.

[7]Sharp, Kimberly Clark. *After the Light.* New York: William Morrow and Company, 1995.

[8]Ibid., pp. 138-39.

[9]Smoot, George and Keay Davidson. *Wrinkles in Time.* New York: Avon Books, 1993, p. 12.

[10]Johnson, George. *Fire in the Mind.* New York: Vintage Books, 1995, p. 77.

[11]Ibid., p. 78.

[12]Smoot, George and Keay Davidson, op. cit., p. 171.

[13]Wolf, Ph.D., Fred Alan. *The Spiritual Universe.* New York: Simon & Schuster, 1996, p. 70.

[14]The electromagnetic force interacts with electrically charged particles. The weak nuclear force is responsible for radioactivity. The strong nuclear force binds quarks together in the proton and neutron.

[15]Kaku, Michio. *Hyperspace.* New York: Oxford University Press, 1994, pp. 121-24.

[16]Ibid., pp. 99-104.

[17]Ibid., p. 98.

[18]Ibid., pp. 131-32.

[19]Ibid., pp. 151-77.

[20]These numbers are derived from research on the superstring (consistent only in nine spatial dimensions) and the bosonic

string (consistent only in twenty-five spatial dimensions). [Kaku, Michio. *Hyperspace.* New York: Oxford University Press, 1994, p. 168].

[21]Kaku, op. cit., pp. 168-9.
[22]Sharp, op. cit.
[23]Van Pragh, James. *Talking to Heaven.* New York: Signet Books, 1997, p. 3.
[24]Ibid., p. 3.
[25]Johnson, op. cit., p. 81.
[26]Moody, Jr., M.D., Raymond A. *Reflections on Life After Life.* New York: Bantam Books, 1977, p. 18.
[27]Ibid., pp. 19-20.
[28]Ibid., p. 21.
[29]Ibid., p. 22.
[30]Kaku, op. cit., p. 49.
[31]Evans-Wentz, W.Y. (ed.). *The Tibetan Book of the Dead.* New York: Oxford University Press, 1960, p. xlv.
[32]Ibid., pp. xlv-xlvii.
[33]Ibid., p. xlvi.

*Chapter 7: Understanding the Bible*

[1]Barrow, John D. *Theories of Everything.* New York: Fawcett Columbine, 1991, pp. 36-7.
[2]Schroeder, Gerald L. *The Science of God.* New York: Free Press, 1997, pp. 24-5.
[3]Barrow, op. cit., pp. 33-4.
[4]Schroeder, op. cit., p. 51.
[5]Ibid., pp. 50-66.
[6]Ibid., p. 66.
[7]Arms, Karen and Pamela S. Camp. *Biology A Journey into Life.* Philadelphia: Saunders College Publishing, 1988, p. 279.
[8]Ibid., pp. 281-82.
[9]Schroeder, op. cit., p. 95.
[10]The logarithmic scale, which Schroeder employs, is the natural log e, required to match the exponential slowing of time as the universe expanded.
[11]Adapted from Schroeder, op. cit., pp. 60, 67.
[12]Arms, op. cit., p. 322.
[13]Ibid., pp. 249-51.

[14]Schroeder, op. cit., p. 129.

[15]Johnson, George. *Fire in the Mind*. New York: Vintage Books, 1995, p. 217.

[16]Lehninger, Albert L. *Biochemistry*. New York: Worth Publishers, Inc., 1970, p. 73.

[17]Johnson, op. cit., p. 217.

[18]Arms, op. cit., pp. 156-67.

[19]Ibid., p. 51.

[20]Goldsborough, Reid. "Deep Blue's Successor to Probe Human Body." *Physicians Financial News*. 28 Feb. 2000: 23.

[21]Schroeder, op. cit., pp. 84-5.

[22]Ibid., pp. 84-5.

[23]Simpson, George Gaylord and William S. Beck. *Life: An Introduction to Biology*. New York: Harcourt, Brace & World, Inc., 1965, p. 760.

[24]Schroeder, op. cit., p. 129.

[25]Ibid., p. 111.

[26]Arms, op. cit., p. 282.

[27]Schroeder, op. cit., p. 113.

[28]Ibid., p. 16.

[29]Ibid., p. 16.

[30]Ibid., p. 121.

[31]Ibid., p. 123.

[32]In August 1996, NASA's announcement of evidence of life in a Martian meteorite added a new perspective to the evolution of life on Earth. Since its finding, scientists must now seriously contemplate that life may have originated from outside our planet.

[33]Schroeder, op. cit., p. 15.

[34]Ibid., pp. 15-6.

[35]Arms, op. cit., p. 251.

[36]Schroeder, op. cit., p. 15.

[37]Peck, M.D., M. Scott. *The Different Drum*. New York: Simon and Schuster, 1987, p. 38.

[38]Harrelson, Walter. *Interpreting the Old Testament*. Chicago: Holt, Rinehart and Winston, Inc., 1964, p. 458.

[39]Harrelson, op. cit., p. 458.

[40]Schroeder, op. cit., p. 99.

[41]Harrelson, op. cit., p. 85.

[42]Ibid., p. 85.

[43]Ellison, H. L., "Genesis" Chapters 1-11, Howley, G.C.D., F.F. Brice, H.L. Ellison (editors). *The New Layman's Bible Commentary*. Grand Rapids: Zondervan Publishing House, 1979, p. 142.

[44]Payne, D. F., "Genesis" Chapters 12-50, Howley, G.C.D., F.F. Brice, H.L. Ellison (editors). *The New Layman's Bible Commentary*. Grand Rapids: Zondervan Publishing House, 1979, p. 149.

[45]Gordon, Robert P., "Exodus", Howley, G.C.D., F.F. Brice, H.L. Ellison (editors). *The New Layman's Bible Commentary*. Grand Rapids: Zondervan Publishing House, 1979, p. 179.

[46]Ibid., p. 183.

[47]Harrelson, op. cit., pp. 82-3.

[48]Gordon, op. cit., p. 189.

[49]Harrelson, op. cit., p. 87.

[50]Gordon, op. cit., p. 189.

[51]Harrelson, op. cit., p. 89.

[52]Moody, Jr., M.D., Raymond A. *Reflections on Life After Life*. New York: Bantam Books, 1977, p. 23.

[53]Ibid., p. 23.

[54]Ibid., pp. 23-24.

[55]Ibid., pp. 26-27.

[56]Ibid., p. 27.

[57]Kushner, Harold S. *When Bad Things Happen to Good People*. New York: Schocken Books, 1981, p. 55.

[58]Fleming, Donald. C., "Ecclesiastes", Howley, G. C. D., F. F. Brice, H. L. Ellison (editors). *The New Layman's Bible Commentary*. Grand Rapids: Zondervan Publishing House, 1979, pp. 742-43.

[59]Clines, David J. A., "Job", Howley, G.C.D., F.F. Brice, H.L. Ellison (editors). *The New Layman's Bible Commentary*. Grand Rapids: Zondervan Publishing House, 1979, p. 559.

[60]Harrelson, op. cit., p. 434.

[61]Peck, M.D., M. Scott. *People of the Lie*. New York: Touchstone Books (Simon and Schuster), 1983, p. 183.

[62]Ibid., pp. 192-3.

[63]Ibid., p. 194.

[64]Ibid., p. 183.

[65]Ibid., p. 184.
[66]Ibid., pp. 189-202.
[67]Ibid., pp. 186-98.
[68]Ibid., p. 200.
[69]Peck, *The Different Drum*, p. 99.
[70]Adapted from Peck, *The Different Drum*, p. 188.
[71]Ibid., p. 189.
[72]Ibid., p. 190.
[73]Ibid., pp. 191-2.
[74]Ibid., p. 192.

### Chapter 8: The Grand Design

[1]Davies, Paul. *About Time*. New York: Touchstone Books, 1995, pp. 146-49.
[2]Davies, Paul. *God & the New Physics*. New York: Touchstone Books, 1983, p. 171.
[3]Gingerich, Owen. "Dare a Scientist Believe in Design?" Templeton, John Marks, editor. *Evidence of Purpose*. New York: Continuum Publishing Co., 1994, p. 23.
[4]Hawking, Stephen. *Black Holes and Baby Universes and Other Essays*. New York: Bantam Books, 1993, p. 150.
[5]Davies, Paul. *The Last Three Minutes*. USA: Basic Books, 1994, p. 45.
[6]Polkingborne, John. "A Potent Universe" Templeton, John Marks, editor. *Evidence of Purpose*. New York: Continuum Publishing Co., 1994, pp. 109-11.
[7]Gingerich, op. cit., p. 24.
[8]Davies, Paul. "The Unreasonable Effectiveness of Science" Templeton, John Marks, editor. *Evidence of Purpose*. New York: Continuum Publishing Co., 1994, p. 49. The interested reader may also wish to refer to his book, *The Accidental Universe*.
[9]Davies, *God & the New Physics*, 1983, p. 188.
[10]Ibid., pp. 178-9.
[11]Schroeder, Gerald L. *The Science of God*. New York: Free Press, 1997, p. 186.
[12]Crick, Francis. *Life Itself*. New York: Simon and Schuster, 1981, p. 88.
[13]Davies, "The Unreasonable Effectiveness of Science", p. 49.
[14]Davies, *God & the New Physics*, p. 187.

[15]Eccles, John C. "The Evolution of Purpose" Templeton, John Marks, editor. *Evidence of Purpose*. New York: Continuum Publishing Co., 1994, p. 132.

[16]Gingerich, op. cit., p. 32.

[17]Osmond, Daniel H. "A Physiologist Looks at Purpose and Meaning in Life." Templeton, John Marks, editor. *Evidence of Purpose*. New York: Continuum Publishing Co., 1994, p. 167.

[18]Polkingborne, John. "A Potent Universe," op. cit., p. 115.

[19]Russell, Robert J. "Cosmology: Evidence for God or Partner for Theology" Templeton, John Marks, editor. *Evidence of Purpose*. New York: Continuum Publishing Co., 1994, p. 90.

[20]Stannard, Russell. "God's Purpose in and Beyond Time" Templeton, John Marks, editor. *Evidence of Purpose*. New York: Continuum Publishing Co., 1994, p. 43.

[21]Templeton, John Marks (ed.). *Evidence of Purpose*. New York: Continuum Publishing Co., 1994, p. 20.

[22]Hawking, op. cit., p. 98.

### Chapter 9; End of Existence

[1]Schroeder, Gerald L. *The Science of God*. New York: Free Press, 1997, p. 185.

[2]Chartrand, Mark R. *National Audubon Society Field Guide to the Night Sky*. New York: Alfred A. Knopf, Inc., 1991, p. 668.

[3]Chartrand, op. cit., pp. 641-71.

[4]A hypothetical particle with zero charge and rest mass that is held to be the quantum of the gravitational field (*Merriam-Webster's Collegiate Dictionary*. Springfield, MA: Merriam-Webster, Inc., 1993, p. 510) .

[5]Davies, Paul. *The Last Three Minutes*. USA: Basic Books, 1994, pp. 57-8.

[6]Hawking, Stephen. *Black Holes and Baby Universes and Other Essays*, op. cit., p. 151.

[7]Ibid., pp. 96-7.

[8]Hawking, Stephen. *A Brief History of Time*. New York: Bantam Books, 1988, p. 150.

[9]Davies, Paul. *God & the New Physics*. New York: Touchstone Books, 1983, p. 178.

[10]Penrose, Roger. *The Emperor's New Mind*. New York: Penguin Books, 1989, p. 317.

[11]Zukav, Gary. *The Dancing Wu Li Masters*. New York: Bantam Books, 1979, p. 222.

[12]Davies, *God & the New Physics*, op. cit., p. 202.

[13]Ibid., op. cit., p. 172.

[14]Davies, *The Last Three Minutes*, op. cit., p 142.

*Chapter 10: Conclusions*

[1]Greene, Brian. *The Elegant Universe*. New York: Vintage Books, 1999, p. 349.

[2]Sharp, Kimberly Clark. *After the Light*. New York: William Morrow and Company, 1995, p. 26.

# References and Suggested Readings

Arms, Karen and Pamela S. Camp. *Biology A Journey into Life.* Philadelphia: Saunders College Publishing, 1988.

Barrow, John D. *Theories of Everything.* New York: Fawcett Columbine, 1991.

*Bible,* Revised Standard Version.

*Book of Mormon.* Salt Lake City: The Church of Jesus Christ of Latter-Day Saints, 1981.

Calder, Nigel. *Einstein's Universe.* New York: Greenwich House, 1979.

Capra, Fritjof. *The Tao of Physics.* Boston: Shambhala Publications, 1991.

Chartrand, Mark R. *National Audubon Society Field Guide to the Night Sky.* New York: Alfred A. Knopf, Inc., 1991.

Cramer, John. "The Transactional Interpretation of Quantum Mechanics," *Reviews of Modern Physics.* 1986; 58(3): 647-687.

Crick, Francis. *Life Itself.* New York: Simon and Schuster, 1981.

Davies, Paul. *About Time.* New York: Touchstone Books, 1995.

———. *God & the New Physics.* New York: Touchstone Books, 1983.

———. *The Last Three Minutes.* USA: Basic Books, 1994..

Dawood, N.J. (translator). *The Koran.* New York: Penguin Books, 1997.

Dressler, Alan. *Voyage to the Great Attractor.* New York: Borzoi Books, 1994.

Edgerton, Franklin (translator). *The Bhagavad Gita.* New York: Harper Torchbooks, 1944.

Evans-Wentz, W.Y. (editor). *The Tibetan Book of the Dead.* New York: Oxford University Press, 1960.

Feynman, Richard P. *The Meaning of It All.* Reading, Massachusetts: Helix Books, 1998.

Fritzsch, Harald. *Quarks.* USA: Basic Books, 1983.

Goldsborough, Reid. "Deep Blue's Successor to Probe Human Body." *Physicians Financial News.* 28 Feb. 2000: 23.

Goodspeed, Edgar J. (translator). *The Apocrypha.* New York: Vintage Books, 1959.

Goswami, Ph.D., Amit, with Richard E. Reed and Maggie Goswami. *The Self-Aware Universe.* New York: Jeremy P. Tarcher/Putnam, 1993.

Greene, Brian. *The Elegant Universe*. New York: Vintage Books, 1999.

Gribbin, John. *In Search of Schrodinger's Cat*. New York: Bantam Books, 1984.

———. *Schrodinger's Kittens and the Search for Reality*. New York: Back Bay Books, 1995.

Harrelson, Walter. *Interpreting the Old Testament*. Chicago: Holt, Rinehart and Winston, Inc., 1964.

Hawking, Stephen. *A Brief History of Time*. New York: Bantam Books, 1988.

———. *Black Holes and Baby Universes and Other Essays*. New York: Bantam Books, 1993.

Herbert, Nick. *Quantum Reality*. New York: Anchor Books, 1985.

Hoffmann, Banesh. *Albert Einstein, Creator and Rebel*. New York: Plume Books, 1972.

*Home Religious Library*. Nashville: The Southwestern Company, 1977.

Howley, G.C.D., F.F. Brice, H.L. Ellison (editors). *The New Layman's Bible Commentary*. Grand Rapids: Zondervan Publishing House, 1979.

Johnson, George. *Fire in the Mind*. New York: Vintage Books, 1995.

Kaku, Michio. *Hyperspace*. New York: Oxford University Press, 1994.

Kaplan, J.D. (editor). *Dialogues of Plato*. New York: Washington Square Press, 1950.

Kushner, Harold S. *When Bad Things Happen to Good People*. New York: Schocken Books, 1981.

Lehninger, Albert L. *Biochemistry*. New York: Worth Publishers, Inc., 1970.

Matt, Daniel C. *The Essential Kabbalah*. Edison, New Jersey: Castle Books, 1995.

*Merriam Webster's Collegiate Dictionary*. Springfield, MA: Merriam-Webster, Inc., 1993.

Moody, Jr., M.D., Raymond A. *Life After Life*. New York: Bantam Books, 1975.

———. *Reflections on Life After Life*. New York: Bantam Books, 1977.

Morgan, Joseph. *Introduction to University Physics*. Boston:

Allyn and Bacon, Inc., 1969.

Morse, M.D., Melvin, with Paul Perry. *Closer to the Light*. New York: Ivy Books, 1990.

———— *Transformed by the Light*. New York: Villard Books, 1992.

Peck, M.D., M. Scott. *People of the Lie*. New York: Touchstone Books (Simon and Schuster), 1983.

————. *The Different Drum*. New York: Simon and Schuster, 1987.

————. *The Road Less Traveled*. New York: Touchstone Books (Simon and Schuster), 1978.

Penrose, Roger. *The Emperor's New Mind*. New York: Penguin Books, 1989.

Russell, Bertrand. *The ABC of Relativity*. New York: Signet Books, 1958.

Sagan, Carl. *Cosmos*. New York: Ballantine Books, 1980.

Schroeder, Gerald L. *The Science of God*. New York: Free Press, 1997.

Sharp, Kimberly Clark. *After the Light*. New York: William Morrow and Company, 1995.

Simpson, George Gaylord and William S. Beck. *Life: An Introduction to Biology*. New York: Harcourt, Brace & World, Inc., 1965.

Smoot, George and Keay Davidson. *Wrinkles in Time*. New York: Avon Books, 1993.

Sternglass, Ernest J. *Before the Big Bang*. New York: Four Walls Eight Windows, 1997.

Templeton, John Marks (editor). *Evidence of Purpose*. New York: Continuum Publishing Co., 1994.

————. *The Humble Approach*. New York: Continuum Publishing Co., 1995.

Van Pragh, James. *Talking to Heaven*. New York: Signet Books, 1997.

Weinberg, Steven. *Dreams of a Final Theory*. New York: Vintage Books, 1993.

Wolf, Ph.D., Fred Alan. *The Spiritual Universe*. New York: Simon & Schuster, 1996.

Zukav, Gary. *The Dancing Wu Li Masters*. New York: Bantam Books, 1979.

# Index

## DISCOVER HOW THE EDGAR CAYCE MATERIAL CAN HELP YOU!

The Association for Research and Enlightenment, Inc. (A.R.E.®), was founded in 1931 by Edgar Cayce. Its international headquarters are in Virginia Beach, Virginia, where thousands of visitors come year-round. Many more are helped and inspired by A.R.E.'s local activities in their own hometowns or by contact via mail (and now the Internet!) with A.R.E. headquarters.

People from all walks of life, all around the world, have discovered meaningful and life-transforming insights in the A.R.E. programs and materials, which focus on such areas as personal spirituality, holistic health, dreams, family life, finding your best vocation, reincarnation, ESP, meditation, and soul growth in small-group settings. Call us today at our toll-free number:

**1-800-333-4499**

or

Explore our electronic visitors center on the Internet: **http://www.edgarcayce.org.**

We'll be happy to tell you more about how the work of the A.R.E. can help you!

A.R.E.
215 67th Street
Virginia Beach, VA 23451-2061